GLIMPSES OF BENGAL

GLIMPSES OF BENGAL

SELECTED FROM

THE

LETTERS

OF

SIR RABINDRANATH TAGORE

1885 TO 1895

SIR RABINDRANATH TAGORE

GYAN

Published by

GYAN

Gyan Publishing House
5, Ansari Road
Daryaganj, New Delhi-110002
Phone: 011-47034999, 9811692060
E-mail: books@gyanbooks.com

Distribution Network
gyanbooks.com
India, USA, Canada, UK, Australia, France

ISBN: 978-81-212-9280-1 (PB)
First Published, 1921

2nd Impression 2023

Printed at: Gyan Press, Delhi.

GLIMPSES OF BENGAL
Author: RABINDRANATH TAGORE

LETTERS

GLIMPSES OF BENGAL

SELECTED FROM

THE

LETTERS

OF

SIR RABINDRANATH TAGORE

1885 TO 1895

MACMILLAN AND CO., LIMITED
ST. MARTIN'S STREET, LONDON
1921

INTRODUCTION

THE letters translated in this book span the most productive period of my literary life, when, owing to great good fortune, I was young and less known.

Youth being exuberant and leisure ample, I felt the writing of letters other than business ones to be a delightful necessity. This is a form of literary extravagance only possible when a surplus of thought and emotion accumulates. Other forms of literature remain the author's and are made public for his good; letters that have been given to private individuals once for all, are therefore characterised by the more generous abandonment.

It so happened that selected extracts from a large number of such letters found their way back to me years after they had been written. It had been rightly conjectured that they would delight me by bringing to mind the memory of days when, under the shelter of obscurity, I enjoyed the greatest freedom my life has ever known.

Since these letters synchronise with a considerable part of my published writings, I thought their parallel course would broaden my readers' understanding of my poems as a track is widened by retreading the same ground. Such was my justification for publishing them in a book for my countrymen. Hoping that the descriptions of village scenes in Bengal contained in these letters would also be of interest to English readers, the translation of a selection of that selection has been entrusted to one who, among all those whom I know, was best fitted to carry it out.

RABINDRANATH TAGORE.

20th June 1920.

BANDORA, BY THE SEA,
October 1885.

THE unsheltered sea heaves and heaves and blanches into foam. It sets me thinking of some tied-up monster straining at its bonds, in front of whose gaping jaws we build our homes on the shore and watch it lashing its tail. What immense strength, with waves swelling like the muscles of a giant!

From the beginning of creation there has been this feud between land and water: the dry earth slowly and silently adding to its domain and spreading a broader and broader lap for its children; the ocean receding step by step, heaving and sobbing and beating its breast in despair. Remember the sea was once sole monarch, utterly free.

Land rose from its womb, usurped its throne, and ever since the maddened old creature, with hoary crest of foam, wails and laments continually, like King Lear exposed to the fury of the elements.

July 1887.

I am in my twenty-seventh year. This event keeps thrusting itself before my mind—nothing else seems to have happened of late.

But to reach twenty-seven—is that a trifling thing?—to pass the meridian of the twenties on one's progress towards thirty?—thirty—that is to say maturity—the age at which people expect fruit rather than fresh foliage. But, alas, where is the promise of fruit? As I shake my head, it still feels brimful of luscious frivolity, with not a trace of philosophy.

Folk are beginning to complain:

"Where is that which we expected of you—that in hope of which we admired the soft green of the shoot? Are we to put up with immaturity for ever? It is high time for us to know what we shall gain from you. We want an estimate of the proportion of oil which the blindfold, mill-turning, unbiassed critic can squeeze out of you."

It has ceased to be possible to delude these people into waiting expectantly any longer. While I was under age they trustfully gave me credit; it is sad to disappoint them now that I am on the verge of thirty. But what am I to do? Words of wisdom will not come! I am utterly incompetent to provide things that may profit the multitude. Beyond a snatch of song, some tittle-tattle, a little merry fooling, I have been unable to advance. And as the result, those who held high hopes will turn their wrath on me; but did any one ever beg them to nurse these expectations?

Such are the thoughts which assail me since one fine *Bysakh* morning I awoke amidst fresh breeze and light, new leaf and flower, to find that I had stepped into my twenty-seventh year.

SHELIDAH, 1888.

Our house-boat is moored to a sandbank on the farther side of the river. A vast expanse of sand stretches away out of sight on every side, with here and there a streak, as of water, running across, though sometimes what gleams like water is only sand.

Not a village, not a human being, not a tree, not a blade of grass—the only breaks in the monotonous whiteness are gaping cracks which in places show the layer of moist, black clay underneath.

Looking towards the East, there is

endless blue above, endless white beneath. Sky empty, earth empty too —the emptiness below hard and barren, that overhead arched and ethereal—one could hardly find elsewhere such a picture of stark desolation.

But on turning to the West, there is water, the currentless bend of the river, fringed with its high bank, up to which spread the village groves with cottages peeping through—all like an enchanting dream in the evening light. I say "the evening light," because in the evening we wander out, and so that aspect is impressed on my mind.

SHAZADPUR, 1890.

The magistrate was sitting in the verandah of his tent dispensing justice to the crowd awaiting their turns under the shade of a tree. They set my palanquin down right under his nose, and the young Englishman received me courteously. He had very light hair, with darker patches here and there, and a moustache just beginning to show. One might have taken him for a white-haired old man but for his extremely youthful face. I asked him over to dinner, but he said he was due elsewhere to arrange for a pig-sticking party.

As I returned home, great black clouds came up and there was a terrific storm with torrents of rain. I could not touch a book, it was impossible to write, so in the I-know-not-what mood I wandered about from room to room. It had become quite dark, the thunder was continually pealing, the lightning gleaming flash after flash, and every now and then sudden gusts of wind would get hold of the big *lichi* tree by the neck and give its shaggy top a thorough shaking. The hollow in front of the house soon filled with water, and as I paced about, it suddenly struck me that I ought to offer the shelter of the house to the magistrate.

I sent off an invitation; then after investigation I found the only spare room encumbered with a platform of planks hanging from the beams, piled with dirty old quilts and bolsters. Servants' belongings, an excessively grimy mat, hubble-bubble pipes, tobacco, tinder, and two wooden chests littered the floor, besides sundry packing-cases full of useless odds and ends, such as a rusty kettle lid, a bottomless iron stove, a discoloured old nickel teapot, a soup-plate full of treacle blackened with dust. In a corner was a tub for washing dishes, and from nails in the wall hung moist dish-clouts and the cook's livery and skull-cap. The only piece of furniture was a rickety dressing-table with water stains, oil stains, milk stains, black, brown, and white stains, and all kinds of mixed stains. The mirror, detached from it, rested against another wall, and the drawers were receptacles for a miscellaneous assortment of articles from soiled napkins down to bottle wires and dust.

For a moment I was overwhelmed with dismay; then it was a case of—send for the manager, send for the storekeeper, call up all the servants, get hold of extra men, fetch water, put up ladders, unfasten ropes, pull down planks, take away bedding, pick up broken glass bit by bit, wrench nails from the wall one by one.—The chandelier falls and its pieces strew the floor; pick them up again piece by piece.—I myself whisk the dirty mat off the floor and out of the window, dislodging a horde of cockroaches, messmates, who dine off my bread, my treacle, and the polish on my shoes.

The magistrate's reply is brought back; his tent is in an awful state and he is coming at once. Hurry up! Hurry up! Presently comes the shout: "The sahib has arrived." All in a flurry I brush the dust off hair, beard, and the rest of myself, and as I go to receive him in the drawing-room, I try to look as respectable as if I had been reposing there comfortably all the afternoon.

I went through the shaking of hands and conversed with the magistrate outwardly serene; still, misgivings about his accommodation would now and then well up within. When at length I had to show my guest to his room, I found it passable, and if the homeless cockroaches do not tickle the soles of his feet, he may manage to get a night's rest.

KALIGRAM, 1891.

I am feeling listlessly comfortable and delightfully irresponsible.

This is the prevailing mood all round here. There is a river but it has no current to speak of, and, lying snugly tucked up in its coverlet of floating weeds, seems to think—"Since it is possible to get on without getting along, why should I bestir myself to stir?" So the sedge which lines the banks knows hardly any disturbance until the fishermen come with their nets.

Four or five large-sized boats are moored near by, alongside each other. On the upper deck of one the boatman is fast asleep, rolled up in a sheet from head to foot. On another, the boatman—also basking in the sun—leisurely twists some yarn into rope. On the lower deck in a third, an oldish-looking, bare-bodied fellow is leaning over an oar, staring vacantly at our boat.

Along the bank there are various other people, but why they come or go, with the slowest of idle steps, or remain seated on their haunches embracing their knees, or keep on gazing at nothing in particular, no one can guess.

The only signs of activity are to be seen amongst the ducks, who, quacking clamorously, thrust their heads under and bob up again to shake off the water with equal energy, as if they repeatedly tried to explore the mysteries below the surface, and every time, shaking their heads, had to report, "Nothing there! Nothing there!"

The days here drowse all their twelve hours in the sun, and silently sleep away the other twelve, wrapped in the mantle of darkness. The only thing you want to do in a place like this is to gaze and gaze on the landscape, swinging your fancies to and fro, alternately humming a tune and nodding dreamily, as the mother on a winter's noonday, her back to the sun, rocks and croons her baby to sleep.

KALIGRAM, 1891.

Yesterday, while I was giving audience to my tenants, five or six boys made their appearance and stood in a primly proper row before me. Before I could put any question their spokesman, in the choicest of high-flown language, started: "Sire! the grace of the Almighty and the good fortune of your benighted children have once more brought about your lordship's auspicious arrival into this locality." He went on in this strain for nearly half an hour. Here and there he would get his lesson wrong, pause, look up at the sky, correct himself, and then go on again. I gathered that their school was short of benches and stools. "For want of these wood-built seats," as he put it, "we know not where to sit ourselves, where to seat our revered teachers, or what to offer our most respected inspector when he comes on a visit."

I could hardly repress a smile at this torrent of eloquence gushing from such a bit of a fellow, which sounded specially out of place here, where the ryots are given to stating their profoundly vital wants in plain and direct vernacular, of which even the more unusual words get sadly twisted out of shape. The clerks and ryots, however, seemed duly impressed, and likewise envious, as though deploring their parents' omission to endow them with so splendid a means of appealing to the *Zamindar*.

I interrupted the young orator before he had done, promising to arrange for the necessary number of benches and stools. Nothing daunted, he allowed me to have my say, then took up his discourse where he had left it, finished it to the last word, saluted me profoundly, and marched off his contingent. He probably would not have minded had I refused to supply the seats, but after all his trouble in getting it by heart he would have resented bitterly being robbed of any part of his speech. So, though it kept more important business waiting, I had to hear him out.

NEARING SHAZADPUR,
January 1891.

We left the little river of Kaligram, sluggish as the circulation in a dying man, and dropped down the current of a briskly flowing stream which led to a region where land and water seemed to merge in each other, river and bank without distinction of garb, like brother and sister in infancy.

The river lost its coating of sliminess, scattered its current in many directions, and spread out, finally, into a *beel* (marsh), with here a patch of grassy land and there a stretch of transparent water, reminding me of the youth of this globe when through the limitless waters land had just begun to raise its head, the separate provinces of solid and fluid as yet undefined.

Round about where we have moored, the bamboo poles of fishermen are planted. Kites hover ready to snatch up fish from the nets. On the ooze at the water's edge stand the saintly-looking paddy birds in meditation. All kinds of waterfowl abound. Patches of weeds float on the water. Here and there rice-fields, untilled, untended,[1] rise from the moist, clay soil. Mosquitoes swarm over the still waters. . . .

We start again at dawn this morning and pass through Kachikata, where the

[1] On the rich river-side silt, rice seed is simply scattered and the harvest reaped when ripe; nothing else has to be done.

waters of the *beel* find an outlet in a winding channel only six or seven yards wide, through which they rush swiftly. To get our unwieldy house-boat through is indeed an adventure. The current hurries it along at lightning speed, keeping the crew busy using their oars as poles to prevent the boat being dashed against the banks. We thus come out again into the open river.

The sky had been heavily clouded, a damp wind blowing, with occasional showers of rain. The crew were all shivering with cold. Such wet and gloomy days in the cold weather are eminently disagreeable, and I have spent a wretched lifeless morning. At two in the afternoon the sun came out, and since then it has been delightful. The banks are now high and covered with peaceful groves and the dwellings of men, secluded and full of beauty.

The river winds in and out, an unknown little stream in the inmost *zenana* of Bengal, neither lazy nor fussy ; lavishing the wealth of her affection on both sides, she prattles about common joys and sorrows and the household news of the village girls, who come for water, and sit by her side, assiduously rubbing their bodies to a glowing freshness with their moistened towels.

This evening we have moored our boat in a lonely bend. The sky is clear. The moon is at its full. Not another boat is to be seen. The moonlight glimmers on the ripples. Solitude reigns on the banks. The distant village sleeps, nestling within a thick fringe of trees. The shrill, sustained chirp of the cicadas is the only sound.

SHAZADPUR,
February 1891.

Just in front of my window, on the other side of the stream, a band of gypsies have ensconced themselves, putting up bamboo frameworks covered over with split-bamboo mats and pieces of cloth. There are only three of these little structures, so low that you cannot stand upright inside. Their life is lived in the open, and they only creep under these shelters at night, to sleep huddled together.

That is always the gypsies' way: no home anywhere, no landlord to pay rent to, wandering about as it pleases them with their children, their pigs, and a dog or two; and on them the police keep a vigilant eye.

I frequently watch the doings of the family nearest me. They are dark but good-looking, with fine, strongly-built bodies, like north-west country folk. Their women are handsome, and have tall, slim, well-knit figures; and with their free and easy movements, and natural independent airs, they look to me like swarthy Englishwomen.

The man has just put the cooking-pot on the fire, and is now splitting bamboos and weaving baskets. The woman first holds up a little mirror to her face, then puts a deal of pains into wiping and rubbing it, over and over again, with a moist piece of cloth; and then, the folds of her upper garment adjusted and tidied, she goes, all spick and span, up to her man and sits beside him, helping him now and then in his work.

These are truly children of the soil, born on it somewhere, bred by the wayside, here, there, and everywhere, dying anywhere. Night and day under the open sky, in the open air, on the bare ground, they lead a unique kind of life; and yet work, love, children, and household duties—everything is there.

They are not idle for a moment, but always doing something. Her own particular task over, one woman plumps herself down behind another, unties the knot of her hair and cleans and arranges it for her; and whether at the same time they fall to talking over the domestic affairs of the three little mat-covered households I cannot say for certain from this distance, but shrewdly suspect it.

This morning a great disturbance invaded the peaceful gypsy settlement. It was about half-past eight or nine. They were spreading out over the mat roofs tattered quilts and sundry other rags, which serve them for beds, in order to sun and air them. The pigs with their litters, lying in a hollow all of a heap and looking like a dab of mud, had been routed out by the two canine members of the family, who fell upon them and sent them roaming in search of their breakfasts, squealing their annoyance at being interrupted in enjoyment of the sun after the cold night. I was writing my letter and absently looking out now and then when the hubbub suddenly commenced.

I rose and went to the window, and found a crowd gathered round the gypsy hermitage. A superior-looking personage was flourishing a stick and indulging in the strongest language. The headman of the gypsies, cowed and nervous, was apparently trying to offer explanations. I gathered that some suspicious happenings in the locality had led to this visitation by a police officer.

The woman, so far, had remained sitting, busily scraping lengths of split bamboo as serenely as if she had been alone and no sort of row going on. Suddenly, however, she sprang to her feet, advanced on the police officer, gesticulated violently with her arms right in his face, and gave him, in strident tones, a piece of her mind. In the twinkling of an eye three-quarters of the officer's excitement had subsided;

he tried to put in a word or two of mild protest but did not get a chance, and so departed crestfallen, a different man.

After he had retreated to a safe distance, he turned and shouted back: "All I say is, you'll have to clear out from here!"

I thought my neighbours opposite would forthwith pack up their mats and bamboos and move away with their bundles, pigs, and children. But there is no sign of it yet. They are still nonchalantly engaged in splitting bamboos, cooking food, or completing a toilet.

SHAZADPUR,
February 1891.

The post office is in a part of our estate office building,—this is very convenient, for we get our letters as soon as they arrive. Some evenings the postmaster comes up to have a chat with me. I enjoy listening to his yarns.

He talks of the most impossible things in the gravest possible manner.

Yesterday he was telling me in what great reverence people of this locality hold the sacred river Ganges. If one of their relatives dies, he said, and they have not the means of taking the ashes to the Ganges, they powder a piece of bone from his funeral pyre and keep it till they come across some one who, some time or other, has drunk of the Ganges. To him they administer some of this powder, hidden in the usual offering of *pán*,[1] and thus are content to imagine that a portion of the remains of their deceased relative has gained purifying contact with the sacred water.

I smiled as I remarked: "This surely must be an invention."

He pondered deeply before he admitted after a pause: "Yes, it may be."

[1] Spices wrapped in betel leaf.

ON THE WAY,
February 1891.

We have got past the big rivers and just turned into a little one.

The village women are standing in the water, bathing or washing clothes; and some, in their dripping *saris*, with veils pulled well over their faces, move homeward with their water vessels filled and clasped against the left flank, the right arm swinging free. Children, covered all over with clay, are sporting boisterously, splashing water on each other, while one of them shouts a song, regardless of the tune.

Over the high banks, the cottage roofs and the tops of the bamboo clumps are visible. The sky has cleared and the sun is shining. Remnants of clouds cling to the horizon like fluffs of cotton wool. The breeze is warmer.

There are not many boats in this little river; only a few dinghies, laden with dry branches and twigs, are moving leisurely along to the tired plash! plash! of their oars. At the river's edge the fishermen's nets are hung out to dry between bamboo poles. And work everywhere seems to be over for the day.

CHUHALI,
June 1891.

I had been sitting out on the deck for more than a quarter of an hour when heavy clouds rose in the west. They came up, black, tumbled, and tattered, with streaks of lurid light showing through here and there. The little boats scurried off into the smaller arm of the river and clung with their anchors safely to its banks. The reapers took up the cut sheaves on their heads and hied homewards; the cows followed, and behind them frisked the calves waving their tails.

Then came an angry roar. Torn-off

scraps of cloud hurried up from the west, like panting messengers of evil tidings. Finally, lightning and thunder, rain and storm, came on altogether and executed a mad dervish dance. The bamboo clumps seemed to howl as the raging wind swept the ground with them, now to the east, now to the west. Over all, the storm droned like a giant snake-charmer's pipe, and to its rhythm swayed hundreds and thousands of crested waves, like so many hooded snakes. The thunder was incessant, as though a whole world was being pounded to pieces away there behind the clouds.

With my chin resting on the ledge of an open window facing away from the wind, I allowed my thoughts to take part in this terrible revelry; they leapt into the open like a pack of schoolboys suddenly set free. When, however, I got a thorough drenching from the spray of the rain, I had to shut up the window and my poetising, and retire quietly into the darkness inside, like a caged bird.

SHAZADPUR,
June 1891.

From the bank to which the boat is tied a kind of scent rises out of the grass, and the heat of the ground, given off in gasps, actually touches my body. I feel that the warm, living Earth is breathing upon me, and that she, also, must feel my breath.

The young shoots of rice are waving in the breeze, and the ducks are in turn thrusting their heads beneath the water and preening their feathers. There is no sound save the faint, mournful creaking of the gangway against the boat, as she imperceptibly swings to and fro in the current.

Not far off there is a ferry. A motley crowd has assembled under the banyan tree awaiting the boat's return; and as soon as it arrives, they eagerly scramble in. I enjoy watching this for hours together. It is market-day in the village on the other bank; that is why the ferry is so busy. Some carry bundles of hay, some baskets, some sacks; some are going to the market, others coming from it. Thus, in this silent noonday, the stream of human activity slowly flows across the river between two villages.

I sat wondering: Why is there always this deep shade of melancholy over the fields and river banks, the sky and the sunshine of our country? And I came to the conclusion that it is because with us Nature is obviously the more important thing. The sky is free, the fields limitless; and the sun merges them into one blazing whole. In the midst of this, man seems so trivial. He comes and goes, like the ferry-boat, from this shore to the other; the babbling hum of his talk, the fitful echo of his song, is heard; the slight movement of his pursuit of his own petty desires is seen in the world's market-places: but how feeble, how temporary, how tragically meaningless it all seems amidst the immense aloofness of the Universe!

The contrast between the beautiful, broad, unalloyed peace of Nature—calm, passive, silent, unfathomable,—and our own everyday worries—paltry, sorrow-laden, strife-tormented, puts me beside myself as I keep staring at the hazy, distant, blue line of trees which fringe the fields across the river.

Where Nature is ever hidden, and cowers under mist and cloud, snow and darkness, there man feels himself master; he regards his desires, his works, as permanent; he wants to perpetuate them, he looks towards posterity, he raises monuments, he writes biographies; he even goes the length of erecting tombstones over the dead. So busy is he that he has not time to consider how many monuments crumble, how often names are forgotten!

SHAZADPUR,
June 1891.

There was a great, big mast lying on the river bank, and some little village urchins, with never a scrap of clothing, decided, after a long consultation, that if it could be rolled along to the accompaniment of a sufficient amount of vociferous clamour, it would be a new and altogether satisfactory kind of game. The decision was no sooner come to than acted upon, with a "*Shabash*, brothers! All together! Heave ho!" And at every turn it rolled, there was uproarious laughter.

The demeanour of one girl in the party was very different. She was playing with the boys for want of other companions, but she clearly viewed with disfavour these loud and strenuous games. At last she stepped up to the mast and, without a word, deliberately sat on it.

So rare a game to come to so abrupt a stop! Some of the players seemed to resign themselves to giving it up as a bad job; and retiring a little way off, they sulkily glared at the girl in her impassive gravity. One made as if he would push her off, but even this did not disturb the careless ease of her pose. The eldest lad came up to her and pointed to other equally suitable places for taking a rest; at which she energetically shook her head, and putting her hands in her lap, steadied herself down still more firmly on her seat. Then at last they had recourse to physical argument and were completely successful.

Once again joyful shouts rent the skies, and the mast rolled along so gloriously that even the girl had to cast aside her pride and her dignified exclusiveness and make a pretence of joining in the unmeaning excitement. But one could see all the time that she was sure boys never know how to play properly, and are always so childish! If only she had the regulation yellow earthen doll handy, with its big, black top-knot, would she ever have deigned to join in this silly game with these foolish boys?

All of a sudden the idea of another splendid pastime occurred to the boys. Two of them got hold of a third by the arms and legs and began to swing him. This must have been great fun, for they all waxed enthusiastic over it. But it was more than the girl could stand, so she disdainfully left the playground and marched off home.

Then there was an accident. The boy who was being swung was let fall. He left his companions in a pet, and went and lay down on the grass with his arms crossed under his head, desiring to convey thereby that never again would he have anything to do with this bad, hard world, but would forever lie, alone by himself, with his arms under his head, and count the stars and watch the play of the clouds.

The eldest boy, unable to bear the idea of such untimely world-renunciation, ran up to the disconsolate one and taking his head on his own knees repentantly coaxed him. "Come, my little brother! Do get up, little brother! Have we hurt you, little brother?" And before long I found them playing, like two pups, at catching and snatching away each other's hands! Two minutes had hardly passed before the little fellow was swinging again.

SHAZADPUR,
June 1891.

I had a most extraordinary dream last night. The whole of Calcutta seemed enveloped in some awful mystery, the houses being only dimly visible through a dense, dark mist, within the veil of which there were strange doings.

I was going along Park Street in a hackney carriage, and as I passed St. Xavier's College I found it had started growing rapidly and was fast getting impossibly high within its enveloping haze. Then it was borne in on me that a band of magicians had come to Calcutta who, if they were paid for it, could bring about many such wonders.

When I arrived at our Jorasanko house, I found these magicians had turned up there too. They were ugly-looking, of a Mongolian type, with scanty moustaches and a few long hairs sticking out of their chins. They could make men grow. Some of the girls wanted to be made taller, and the magician sprinkled some powder over their heads and they promptly shot up. To every one I met I kept repeating: "This is most extraordinary,—just like a dream!"

Then some one proposed that our house should be made to grow. The magicians agreed, and as a preliminary began to take down some portions. The dismantling over, they demanded money, or else they would not go on. The cashier strongly objected. How could payment be made before the work was completed? At this the magicians got wild and twisted up the building most fearsomely, so that men and brick-work got mixed together, bodies inside walls and only head and shoulders showing.

It had altogether the look of a thoroughly devilish business, as I told my eldest brother. "You see," said I, "the kind of thing it is. We had better call upon God to help us!" But try as I might to anathematise them in the name of God, my heart felt like breaking and no words would come. Then I awoke.

A curious dream, was it not? Calcutta in the hands of Satan and growing diabolically, within the darkness of an unholy mist!

SHAZADPUR,
June 1891.

The schoolmasters of this place paid me a visit yesterday.

They stayed on and on, while for the life of me I could not find a word to say. I managed a question or so every five minutes, to which they offered the briefest replies; and then I sat vacantly, twirling my pen, and scratching my head.

At last I ventured on a question about the crops, but being schoolmasters they knew nothing whatever about crops.

About their pupils I had already asked them everything I could think of, so I had to start over again: How many boys had they in the school? One said eighty, another said a hundred and seventy-five. I hoped that this might lead to an argument, but no, they made up their difference.

Why, after an hour and a half, they should have thought of taking leave, I cannot tell. They might have done so with as good a reason an hour earlier, or, for the matter of that, twelve hours later! Their decision was clearly arrived at empirically, entirely without method.

SHAZADPUR,
July 1891.

There is another boat at this landing-place, and on the shore in front of it a crowd of village women. Some are evidently embarking on a journey and the others seeing them off; infants, veils, and grey hairs are all mixed up in the gathering.

One girl in particular attracts my attention. She must be about eleven or twelve; but, buxom and sturdy, she might pass for fourteen or fifteen. She has a winsome face—very dark, but very pretty. Her hair is cut short like a boy's, which well becomes her simple, frank, and alert expression. She has a child in her arms and is staring at me with unabashed curiosity, and certainly no lack of straightforwardness or intelligence in her glance. Her half-boyish, half-girlish manner is singularly attractive—a novel blend of masculine nonchalance and feminine charm. I had no idea there were such types among our village women in Bengal.

None of this family, apparently, is troubled with too much bashfulness. One of them has unfastened her hair in the sun and is combing it out with her fingers, while conversing about their domestic affairs at the top of her voice with another, on board. I gather she has no other children except a girl, a foolish creature who knows neither how to behave or talk, nor even the difference between kin and stranger. I also learn that Gopal's son-in-law has turned out a ne'er-do-well, and that his daughter refuses to go to her husband.

When, at length, it was time to start, they escorted my short-haired damsel, with plump shapely arms, her gold bangles and her guileless, radiant face, into the boat. I could divine that she was returning from her father's to her husband's home. They all stood there, following the boat with their gaze as it cast off, one or two wiping their eyes with the loose end of their *saris*. A little girl, with her hair tightly tied into a knot, clung to the neck of an older woman and silently wept on her shoulder. Perhaps she was losing a darling Didimani[1] who joined in her doll games and also slapped her when she was naughty. . . .

The quiet floating away of a boat on the stream seems to add to the pathos of a separation—it is so like death—the departing one lost to sight, those left behind returning to their daily life, wiping their eyes. True, the pang lasts but a while, and is perhaps already wearing off both in those who have gone and those who remain,—pain being temporary, oblivion permanent. But none the less it is not the forgetting, but the pain which is true; and every now and then, in separation or in death, we realise how terribly true.

[1] An elder sister is often called sister-jewel (*Didimani*).

On board a Canal Steamer
going to Cuttack,
August 1891.

My bag left behind, my clothes daily get more and more intolerably disreputable,—this thought continually uppermost is not compatible with a due sense of self-respect. With the bag I could have faced the world of men head erect and spirits high; without it, I fain would skulk in corners, away from the glances of the crowd. I go to bed in these clothes and in them I appear in the morning, and on the top of that the steamer is full of soot, and the unbearable heat of the day keeps one unpleasantly moist.

Apart from this, I am having quite a time of it on board the steamer. My fellow-passengers are of inexhaustible variety. There is one, Aghore Babu, who cannot allude to anything, animate or inanimate, except in terms of personal abuse. There is another, a lover of music, who persists in attempting variations on the Bhairab[1] mode at dead of night, convincing me of the untimeliness of his performance in more senses than one.

The steamer has been aground in a narrow ditch of a canal ever since last evening, and it is now past nine in the morning. I spent the night in a corner of the crowded deck, more dead than alive. I had asked the steward to fry some *luchis* for my dinner, and he brought me some nondescript slabs of fried dough with no vegetable accompaniments to eat them with. On my expressing a pained surprise, he was all contrition and offered to make me some hotch-potch at once. But the night being already far advanced, I declined his offer, managed to swallow a few

[1] A Raga, or mode of Indian classical music, supposed to be appropriate to the early dawn.

mouthfuls of the stuff dry, and then, all lights on and the deck packed with passengers, laid myself down to sleep.

Mosquitoes hovered above, cockroaches wandered around. There was a fellow-sleeper stretched crosswise at my feet whose body my soles every now and then came up against. Four or five noses were engaged in snoring. Several mosquito-tormented, sleepless wretches were consoling themselves by pulls at their hubble-bubble pipes; and above all, there rose those variations on the mode *Bhairab*! Finally, at half-past three in the morning, some fussy busybodies began loudly inciting each other to get up. In despair, I also left my bed and dropped into my deck-chair to await the dawn. Thus passed that variegated nightmare of a night.

One of the hands tells me that the steamer has stuck so fast that it may take the whole day to get her off. I inquire of another whether any Calcutta-bound steamer will be passing, and get the smiling reply that this is the only boat on this line, and I may come back in her, if I like, after she has reached Cuttack! By a stroke of luck, after a great deal of tugging and hauling, they have just got her afloat at about ten o'clock.

TIRAN,
7th September 1891.

The landing-place at Balia makes a pretty picture with its fine big trees on either side, and on the whole the canal somehow reminds me of the little river at Poona. On thinking it over I am sure I should have liked the canal much better had it really been a river.

Cocoanut palms as well as mangoes and other shady trees line its banks, which, turfed with beautifully green grass, slope gently down to the water, and are sprinkled over with sensitive plants in flower. Here and there are screwpine groves, and through gaps in the border of trees glimpses can be caught of endless fields, stretching away into the distance, their crops so soft and velvety after the rains that the eye seems to sink into their depths. Then again, there are the little villages under their clusters of cocoanut and date palms, nestling under the moist cool shade of the low seasonal clouds.

Through all these the canal, with its gentle current, winds gracefully between its clean, grassy banks, fringed, in its narrower stretches, with clusters of water-lilies with reeds growing among them. And yet the mind keeps fretting at the idea that after all it is nothing but an artificial canal.

The murmur of its waters does not reach back to the beginning of time. It knows naught of the mysteries of some distant, inaccessible mountain cave. It has not flowed for ages, graced with an old-world feminine name, giving the villages on its sides the milk of its breast. Even old artificial lakes have acquired a greater dignity.

However when, a hundred years hence, the trees on its banks will have grown statelier ; its brand-new milestones been worn down and moss-covered into mellowness ; the date 1871, inscribed on its lock-gates, left behind at a respectable distance ; then, if I am reborn as my great-grandson and come again to inspect the Cuttack estates along this canal, I may feel differently towards it.

SHELIDAH,
October 1891.

Boat after boat touches at the landing-place, and after a whole year exiles are returning home from distant fields of work for the Poojah vacation, their boxes, baskets, and bundles loaded with presents. I notice one who, as his boat nears the shore, changes into a freshly folded and crinkled muslin *dhoti*, dons over his cotton tunic a China silk coat, carefully adjusts round his neck a neatly twisted scarf, and walks off towards the village, umbrella held aloft.

Rustling waves pass over the rice-fields. Mango and cocoanut tree-tops rise into the sky, and beyond them there are fluffy clouds on the horizon. The fringes of the palm leaves wave in the breeze. The reeds on the sand-bank are on the point of flowering. It is altogether an exhilarating scene.

The feelings of the man who has just arrived home, the eager expectancy of his folk awaiting him, this autumn sky, this world, the gentle morning breeze, the universal responsive tremor in tree and shrub and in the wavelets on the river, conspire to overwhelm this lonely youth, gazing from his window, with unutterable joys and sorrows.

Glimpses of the world received from wayside windows bring new desires, or rather, make old desires take on new forms. The day before yesterday, as I was sitting at the window of the boat, a little fisher-dinghy floated past, the boatman singing a song—not a very tuneful song. But it reminded me of a night, years ago, when I was a child. We were going along the Padma in a boat. I awoke one night at about 2 o'clock, and, on raising the window and putting out my head, I saw the waters without a ripple, gleaming in the moonlight, and a youth in a little dinghy paddling along all by himself and singing, oh so sweetly,—such sweet melody I had never heard before.

A sudden longing came upon me to go back to the day of that song; to be allowed to make another essay at life, this time not to leave it thus empty and unsatisfied; but with a poet's song on my lips to float about the world on the crest of the rising tide, to sing it to men and subdue their hearts; to see for myself what the world holds and where; to let men know me, to get to know them; to burst forth through the world in life and youth like the eager rushing breezes; and then return home to a fulfilled and fruitful old age to spend it as a poet should.

Not a very lofty ideal, is it? To benefit the world would have been much higher, no doubt; but being on the whole what I am, that ambition does not even occur to me. I cannot make up my mind to sacrifice this precious gift of life in a self-wrought famine, and disappoint the world and the hearts of men by fasts and meditations and constant argument. I count it enough to live and die as a man, loving and trusting the world, unable to look on it either as a delusion of the Creator or a snare of the Devil. It is not for me to strive to be wafted away into the airiness of an Angel.

SHELIDAH,
2nd Kartik (October) 1891.

When I come to the country I cease to view man as separate from the rest. As the river runs through many a clime, so does the stream of men babble on, winding through woods and villages and towns. It is not a true contrast that *men may come and men may go, but I go on for ever.* Humanity, with all its confluent streams, big and small, flows on and on, just as does the river, from its source in birth to its sea of death;—two dark mysteries at either end, and between them various play and work and chatter unceasing.

Over there the cultivators sing in the

fields: here the fishing-boats float by. The day wears on and the heat of the sun increases. Some bathers are still in the river, others are finished and are taking home their filled water-vessels. Thus, past both banks of the river, hundreds of years have hummed their way, while the refrain rises in a mournful chorus: *I go on for ever!*

Amid the noonday silence some youthful cowherd is heard calling at the top of his voice for his companion; some boat splashes its way homewards; the ripples lap against the empty jar which some village woman rests on the water before dipping it; and with these mingle several other less definite sounds,—the twittering of birds, the humming of bees, the plaintive creaking of the house-boat as it gently swings to and fro,—the whole making a tender lullaby, as of a mother trying to quiet a suffering child. "Fret not," she sings, as she soothingly pats its fevered forehead. "Worry not; weep no more. Let be your strugglings and grabbings and fightings; forget a while, sleep a while."

SHELIDAH,
3rd Kartik (October) 1891.

It was the *Kojagar* full moon, and I was slowly pacing the riverside conversing with myself. It could hardly be called a conversation, as I was doing all the talking and my imaginary companion all the listening. The poor fellow had no chance of speaking up for himself, for was not mine the power to compel him helplessly to answer like a fool?

But what a night it was! How often have I tried to write of such, but never got it done! There was not a line of ripple on the river; and from away over there, where the farthest shore of the distant main stream is seen beyond the other edge of the midway belt of sand, right up to this shore, glimmers a broad band of moonlight. Not a human being, not a boat in sight; not a tree, nor blade of grass on the fresh-formed island sand-bank.

It seemed as though a desolate moon was rising upon a devastated earth; a random river wandering through a lifeless solitude; a long-drawn fairy-tale coming to a close over a deserted world, —all the kings and the princesses, their ministers and friends and their golden castles vanished, leaving the Seven Seas and Thirteen Rivers and the Unending Moor, over which the adventurous princes fared forth, wanly gleaming in the pale moonlight. I was pacing up and down like the last pulse-beats of this dying world. Every one else seemed to be on the opposite shore—the shore of life—where the British Government and the Nineteenth

Century hold sway, and tea and cigarettes.

SHELIDAH,
9th January 1892.

For some days the weather here has been wavering between Winter and Spring. In the morning, perhaps, shivers will run over both land and water at the touch of the north wind; while the evening will thrill with the south breeze coming through the moonlight.

There is no doubt that Spring is well on its way. After a long interval the *papiya* once more calls out from the groves on the opposite bank. The hearts of men too are stirred; and after evening falls, sounds of singing are heard in the village, showing that they are no longer in such a hurry to close doors and windows and cover themselves up snugly for the night.

To-night the moon is at its full, and

its large, round face peers at me through the open window on my left, as if trying to make out whether I have anything to say against it in my letter,—it suspects, maybe, that we mortals concern ourselves more with its stains than its beams.

A bird is plaintively crying tee-tee on the sand-bank. The river seems not to move. There are no boats. The motionless groves on the bank cast an unquivering shadow on the waters. The haze over the sky makes the moon look like a sleepy eye kept open.

Henceforward the evenings will grow darker and darker; and when, to-morrow, I come over from the office, this moon, the favourite companion of my exile, will already have drifted a little farther from me, doubting whether she had been wise to lay her heart so completely bare last evening, and so covering it up again little by little.

Nature becomes really and truly intimate in strange and lonely places. I have been actually worrying myself for days at the thought that after the moon is past her full I shall daily miss the moonlight more and more; feeling further and further exiled when the beauty and peace which awaits my return to the riverside will no longer be there, and I shall have to come back through darkness.

Anyhow I put it on record that to-day is the full moon—the first full moon of this year's springtime. In years to come I may perchance be reminded of this night, with the tee-tee of the bird on the bank, the glimmer of the distant light on the boat off the other shore, the shining expanse of river, the blur of shade thrown by the dark fringe of trees along its edge, and the white sky gleaming overhead in unconcerned aloofness.

SHELIDAH,
7th April 1892.

The river is getting low, and the water in this arm of it is hardly more than waist-deep anywhere. So it is not at all extraordinary that the boat should be anchored in mid-stream. On the bank, to my right, the ryots are ploughing and cows are now and then brought down to the water's edge for a drink. To the left there are the mango and cocoanut trees of the old Shelidah garden above, and on the bathing slope below there are village women washing clothes, filling water jars, bathing, laughing and gossiping in their provincial dialect.

The younger girls never seem to get through their sporting in the water; it is a delight to hear their careless, merry laughter. The men gravely take their regulation number of dips and go away, but girls are on much more intimate terms with the water. Both alike babble and chatter and ripple and sparkle in the same simple and natural manner; both may languish and fade away under a scorching glare, yet both can take a blow without hopelessly breaking under it. The hard world, which, but for them, would be barren, cannot fathom the mystery of the soft embrace of their arms.

Tennyson has it that woman to man is as water to wine. I feel to-day it should be as water is to land. Woman is more at home with the water, laving in it, playing with it, holding her gatherings beside it; and while, for her, other burdens are not seemly, the carrying of water from the spring, the well, the bank of river or pool, has ever been held to become her.

Bolpur,
2nd May 1892.

There are many paradoxes in the world and one of them is this, that wherever the landscape is immense, the sky unlimited, clouds intimately dense, feelings unfathomable—that is to say where infinitude is manifest — its fit companion is one solitary person; a multitude there seems so petty, so distracting.

An individual and the infinite are on equal terms, worthy to gaze on one another, each from his own throne. But where many men are, how small both humanity and infinitude become, how much they have to knock off each other, in order to fit in together! Each soul wants so much room to expand that in a crowd it needs must wait for gaps through which to thrust a little craning piece of a head from time to time.

So the only result of our endeavour to assemble is that we become unable to fill our joined hands, our outstretched arms, with this endless, fathomless expanse.

BOLPUR,
8th Jaistha (May) 1892.

Women who try to be witty, but only succeed in being pert, are insufferable; and as for attempts to be comic they are disgraceful in women whether they succeed or fail. The comic is ungainly and exaggerated, and so is in some sort related to the sublime. The elephant is comic, the camel and the giraffe are comic, all overgrowth is comic.

It is rather keenness that is akin to beauty, as the thorn to the flower. So sarcasm is not unbecoming in woman, though coming from her it hurts. But ridicule which savours of bulkiness woman had better leave to our sublime sex. The masculine Falstaff makes our sides split, but a feminine Falstaff would only rack our nerves.

BOLPUR,
12th Jaistha (*May*) 1892.

I usually pace the roof-terrace, alone, of an evening. Yesterday afternoon I felt it my duty to show my visitors the beauties of the local scenery, so I strolled out with them, taking Aghore as a guide.

On the verge of the horizon, where the distant fringe of trees was blue, a thin line of dark blue cloud had risen over them and was looking particularly beautiful. I tried to be poetical and said it was like blue collyrium on the fringe of lashes enhancing a beautiful blue eye. Of my companions one did not hear the remark, another did not understand, while the third dismissed it with the reply: "Yes, very pretty." I did not feel encouraged to attempt a second poetical flight.

After walking about a mile we came to a dam, and along the pool of water there was a row of *tâl* (fan palm) trees, under which was a natural spring. While we stood there looking at this, we found that the line of cloud which we had seen in the North was making for us, swollen and grown darker, flashes of lightning gleaming the while.

We unanimously came to the conclusion that viewing the beauties of nature could be better done from within the shelter of the house, but no sooner had we turned homewards than a storm, making giant strides over the open moorland, was on us with an angry roar. I had no idea, while I was admiring the collyrium on the eyelashes of beauteous dame Nature, that she would fly at us like an irate housewife, threatening so tremendous a slap!

It became so dark with the dust that we could not see beyond a few paces. The fury of the storm increased, and flying stony particles of the rubbly soil stung our bodies like shot, as the wind took us by the scruff of the neck and thrust us along, to the whipping of drops of rain which had begun to fall.

Run! Run! But the ground was not level, being deeply scarred with watercourses, and not easy to cross at any time, much less in a storm. I managed to get entangled in a thorny shrub, and was nearly thrown on my face by the force of the wind as I stopped to free myself.

When we had almost reached the house, a host of servants came hurrying towards us, shouting and gesticulating, and fell upon us like another storm. Some took us by the arms, some bewailed our plight, some were eager to show the way, others hung on our backs as if fearing that the storm might carry us off altogether. We evaded their attentions with some difficulty and managed at length to get into the house, panting, with wet clothes, dusty bodies, and tumbled hair.

One thing I had learnt; and will never again write in novel or story the lie that the hero with the picture of his lady-love in his mind can pass unruffled through wind and rain. No one could keep any face in mind, however lovely, in such a storm,—he has enough to do to keep the sand out of his eyes! . . .

The Vaishnava poets have sung ravishingly of Radha going to her tryst with Krishna through a stormy night. Did they ever pause to consider, I wonder, in what condition she must have reached him? The kind of tangle her hair got into is easily imaginable, and also the state of the rest of her toilet. When she arrived in her bower with the dust on her body soaked by the rain into a coating of mud, she must have been a sight!

But when we read the Vaishnava

poems, these thoughts do not occur. We only see on the canvas of our mind the picture of a beautiful woman, passing under the shelter of the flowering kadambas in the darkness of a stormy *Shravan*[1] night, towards the bank of the Jumna, forgetful of wind or rain, as in a dream, drawn by her surpassing love. She has tied up her anklets lest they should tinkle; she is clad in dark blue raiment lest she be discovered; but she holds no umbrella lest she get wet, carries no lantern lest she fall!

Alas for useful things—how necessary in practical life, how neglected in poetry! But poetry strives in vain to free us from their bondage—they will be with us always; so much so, we are told, that with the march of civilisation it is poetry that will become extinct, but patent after patent will continue to be

[1] July–August, the rainy season.

taken out for the improvement of shoes and umbrellas.

BOLPUR,
16*th Jaistha* (*May*) 1892.

No church tower clock chimes here, and there being no other human habitation near by, complete silence falls with the evening, as soon as the birds have ceased their song. There is not much difference between early night and midnight. A sleepless night in Calcutta flows like a huge, slow river of darkness; one can count the varied sounds of its passing, lying on one's back in bed. But here the night is like a vast, still lake, placidly reposing, with no sign of movement. And as I tossed from side to side last night I felt enveloped within a dense stagnation.

This morning I left my bed a little later than usual and, coming downstairs to my room, leant back on a bolster, one leg resting over the other knee. There, with a slate on my chest, I began to write a poem to the accompaniment of the morning breeze and the singing birds. I was getting along splendidly—a smile playing over my lips, my eyes half closed, my head swaying to the rhythm, the thing I hummed gradually taking shape—when the post arrived.

There was a letter, the last number of the *Sadhana Magazine*, one of the *Monist*, and some proof-sheets. I read the letter, raced my eyes over the uncut pages of the *Sadhana*, and then again fell to nodding and humming through my poem. I did not do another thing till I had finished it.

I wonder why the writing of pages of prose does not give one anything like the joy of completing a single poem. One's emotions take on such perfection of form in a poem; they can, as it were, be taken up by the fingers. But prose is like a sackful of loose material, heavy and unwieldy, incapable of being lifted as you please.

If I could finish writing one poem a day, my life would pass in a kind of joy; but though I have been busy tending poetry for many a year it has not been tamed yet, and is not the kind of winged steed to allow me to bridle it whenever I like! The joy of art is in freedom to take a distant flight as fancy will; then, even after return within the prison-world, an echo lingers in the ear, an exaltation in the mind.

Short poems keep coming to me unsought, and so prevent my getting on with the play. Had it not been for these, I could have let in ideas for two or three plays which have been knocking at the door. I am afraid I must wait for the cold weather. All my plays except "Chitra" were written in the winter. In that season lyrical fervour is apt to grow cold, and one gets the leisure to write drama.

BOLPUR,
31st May 1892.

It is not yet five o'clock, but the light has dawned, there is a delightful breeze, and all the birds in the garden are awake and have started singing. The *koel* seems beside itself. It is difficult to understand why it should keep on cooing so untiringly. Certainly not to entertain us, nor to distract the pining lover[1]—it must have some personal purpose of its own. But, sadly enough, that purpose never seems to get fulfilled. Yet it is not down-hearted, and its Coo-oo! Coo-oo! keeps going, with now and then an ultra-fervent trill. What can it mean?

And then in the distance there is

[1] A favourite conceit of the old Sanskrit poets.

some other bird with only a faint chuck-chuck that has no energy or enthusiasm, as if all hope were lost; none the less, from within some shady nook it cannot resist uttering this little plaint: chuck, chuck, chuck.

How little we really know of the household affairs of these innocent winged creatures, with their soft breasts and necks and their many-coloured feathers! Why on earth do they find it necessary to sing so persistently?

SHELIDAH,
31st Jaistha (June) 1892.

I hate these polite formalities. Nowadays I keep repeating the line: "Much rather would I be an Arab Bedouin!" A fine, healthy, strong, and free barbarity.

I feel I want to quit this constant ageing of mind and body, with incessant argument and nicety concerning ancient decaying things, and to feel the joy of a free and vigorous life; to have,—be they good or bad,—broad, unhesitating, unfettered ideas and aspirations, free from everlasting friction between custom and sense, sense and desire, desire and action.

If only I could set utterly and boundlessly free this hampered life of mine, I would storm the four quarters and raise wave upon wave of tumult all round; I would career away madly, like a wild horse, for very joy of my own speed! But I am a Bengali, not a Bedouin! I go on sitting in my corner, and mope and worry and argue. I turn my mind now this way up, now the other—as a fish is fried—and the boiling oil blisters first this side, then that.

Let it pass. Since I cannot be thoroughly wild, it is but proper that I should make an endeavour to be thoroughly civil. Why foment a quarrel between the two?

SHELIDAH,
16th June 1892.

The more one lives alone on the river or in the open country, the clearer it becomes that nothing is more beautiful or great than to perform the ordinary duties of one's daily life simply and naturally. From the grasses in the field to the stars in the sky, each one is doing just that; and there is such profound peace and surpassing beauty in nature because none of these tries forcibly to transgress its limitations.

Yet what each one does is by no means of little moment. The grass has to put forth all its energy to draw sustenance from the uttermost tips of its rootlets simply to grow where it is as grass; it does not vainly strive to become a banyan tree; and so the earth gains a lovely carpet of green. And, indeed, what little of beauty and peace is to be found in the societies of men is owing to the daily performance of small duties, not to big doings and fine talk.

Perhaps because the whole of our life is not vividly present at each moment, some imaginary hope may lure, some glowing picture of a future, untrammelled with everyday burdens, may tempt us; but these are illusory.

SHELIDAH,
2nd Asarh (June) 1892.

Yesterday, the first day of *Asarh*,[1] the enthronement of the rainy season was celebrated with due pomp and circumstance. It was very hot the whole day, but in the afternoon dense clouds rolled up in stupendous masses.

I thought to myself, this first day of the rains, I would rather risk getting wet than remain confined in my dungeon of a cabin.

[1] June–July, the commencement of the rainy season.

The year 1293[1] will not come again in my life, and, for the matter of that, how many more even of these first days of *Asarh* will come? My life would be sufficiently long could it number thirty of these first days of *Asarh* to which the poet of the *Meghaduta*[2] has, for me at least, given special distinction.

It sometimes strikes me how immensely fortunate I am that each day should take its place in my life, either reddened with the rising and setting sun, or refreshingly cool with deep, dark clouds, or blooming like a white flower in the moonlight. What untold wealth!

A thousand years ago Kalidas welcomed that first day of *Asarh*; and once in every year of my life that same day of *Asarh* dawns in all its glory—

[1] Of the Bengal era.

[2] In the *Meghaduta* (Cloud Messenger) of Kalidas a famous description of the burst of the Monsoon begins with the words: *On the first day of Asarh.*

that self-same day of the poet of old Ujjain, which has brought to countless men and women their joys of union, their pangs of separation.

Every year one such great, time-hallowed day drops out of my life; and the time will come when this day of Kalidas, this day of the *Meghaduta*, this eternal first day of the Rains in Hindustan, shall come no more for me. When I realise this I feel I want to take a good look at nature, to offer a conscious welcome to each day's sunrise, to say farewell to each day's setting sun, as to an intimate friend.

What a grand festival, what a vast theatre of festivity! And we cannot even fully respond to it, so far away do we live from the world! The light of the stars travels millions of miles to reach the earth, but it cannot reach our hearts—so many millions of miles further off are we!

The world into which I have tumbled is peopled with strange beings. They are always busy erecting walls and rules round themselves, and how careful they are with their curtains lest they should see! It is a wonder to me they have not made drab covers for flowering plants and put up a canopy to ward off the moon. If the next life is determined by the desires of this, then I should be reborn from our enshrouded planet into some free and open realm of joy.

Only those who cannot steep themselves in beauty to the full, despise it as an object of the senses. But those who have tasted of its inexpressibility know how far it is beyond the highest powers of mere eye or ear — nay, even the heart is powerless to attain the end of its yearning.

P.S.—I have left out the very thing I started to tell of. Don't be afraid, it won't take four more sheets. It is this, that on the evening of the first day of *Asarh* it came on to rain very heavily, in great lance-like showers. That is all.

ON THE WAY TO GOALUNDA,
21st June 1892.

Pictures in an endless variety, of sand-banks, fields and their crops, and villages, glide into view on either hand — of clouds floating in the sky, of colours blossoming when day meets night. Boats steal by, fishermen catch fish; the waters make liquid, caressing sounds throughout the livelong day; their broad expanse calms down in the evening stillness, like a child lulled to sleep, over whom all the stars in the boundless sky keep watch—then, as I sit up on wakeful nights, with sleeping banks on either side, the silence is broken only by an occasional cry of a jackal in the woods near some village, or by fragments undermined by the keen current of the Padma, that tumble from the high cliff-like bank into the water.

Not that the prospect is always of particular interest — a yellowish sand-bank, innocent of grass or tree, stretches away; an empty boat is tied to its edge; the bluish water, of the same shade as the hazy sky, flows past; yet I cannot tell how it moves me. I suspect that the old desires and longings of my servant-ridden childhood—when in the solitary imprisonment of my room I pored over the *Arabian Nights*, and shared with Sinbad the Sailor his adventures in many a strange land—are not yet dead within me, but are roused at the sight of any empty boat tied to a sand-bank.

If I had not heard fairy tales and read the *Arabian Nights* and *Robinson Crusoe* in childhood, I am sure views of distant banks, or the farther side of wide fields, would not have stirred me so — the whole world, in fact, would have had for me a different appeal.

What a maze of fancy and fact becomes tangled up within the mind of man! The different strands—petty and great—of story and event and picture, how they get knotted together!

SHELIDAH,
22nd June 1892.

Early this morning, while still lying in bed, I heard the women at the bathing-place sending forth joyous peals of *Ulu! Ulu!*[1] The sound moved me curiously, though it is difficult to say why.

Perhaps such joyful outbursts put one in mind of the great stream of festive activity which goes on in this world, with most of which the individual man has

[1] A peculiar shrill cheer given by women on auspicious or festive occasions.

no connection. The world is so immense, the concourse of men so vast, yet with how few has one any tie! Distant sounds of life, wafted near, bearing tidings from unknown homes, make the individual realise that the greater part of the world of men does not, cannot own or know him; then he feels deserted, loosely attached to the world, and a vague sadness creeps over him.

Thus these cries of *Ulu! Ulu!* made my life, past and future, seem like a long, long road, from the very ends of which they come to me. And this feeling colours for me the beginning of my day.

As soon as the manager with his staff, and the ryots seeking audience, come upon the scene, this faint vista of past and future will be promptly elbowed out, and a very robust present will salute and stand before me.

SHAZADPUR,
25th June 1892.

In to-day's letters there was a touch about A——'s singing which made my heart yearn with a nameless longing. Each of the little joys of life, which remain unappreciated amid the hubbub of the town, send in their claims to the heart when far from home. I love music, and there is no dearth of voices and instruments in Calcutta, yet I turn a deaf ear to them. But, though I may fail to realise it at the time, this needs must leave the heart athirst.

As I read to-day's letters, I felt such a poignant desire to hear A——'s sweet song, I was at once sure that one of the many suppressed longings of creation which cry after fulfilment is for neglected joys within reach; while we are busy pursuing chimerical impossibilities we famish our lives. . . .

The emptiness left by easy joys, untasted, is ever growing in my life. And the day may come when I shall feel that, could I but have the past back, I would strive no more after the unattainable, but drain to the full these little, unsought, everyday joys which life offers.

SHAZADPUR,
27th June 1892.

Yesterday, in the afternoon, it clouded over so threateningly, I felt a sense of dread. I do not remember ever to have seen before such angry-looking clouds.

Swollen masses of the deepest indigo blue were piled, one on top of the other, just above the horizon, looking like the puffed-out moustaches of some raging demon.

Under the jagged lower edges of the clouds there shone forth a blood-red glare, as through the eyes of a monstrous, sky-filling bison, with tossing mane and with head lowered to strike the earth in fury.

The crops in the fields and the leaves of the trees trembled with fear of the impending disaster; shudder after shudder ran across the waters; the crows flew wildly about, distractedly cawing.

SHAZADPUR,
29th June 1892.

I wrote yesterday that I had an engagement with Kalidas, the poet, for this evening. As I lit a candle, drew my chair up to the table, and made ready, not Kalidas, but the postmaster, walked in. A live postmaster cannot but claim precedence over a dead poet, so I could not very well tell him to make way for Kalidas, who was due by appointment,—he would not have understood me! Therefore I offered him a chair and gave old Kalidas the go-by.

There is a kind of bond between this

postmaster and me. When the post office was in a part of this estate building, I used to meet him every day. I wrote my story of "The Postmaster" one afternoon in this very room. And when the story was out in the *Hitabadi* he came to me with a succession of bashful smiles, as he deprecatingly touched on the subject. Anyhow, I like the man. He has a fund of anecdote which I enjoy listening to. He has also a sense of humour.

Though it was late when the postmaster left, I started at once on the *Raghuvansa*,[1] and read all about the *swayamuara*[2] of Indumati.

The handsome, gaily adorned princes are seated on rows of thrones in the assembly hall. Suddenly a blast of

[1] Book of poems by Kalidas, who is perhaps best known to European readers as the author of *Sakuntala*.

[2] An old Indian custom, according to which a princess chooses among assembled rival suitors for her hand by placing a garland round the neck of the one whose love she returns.

conch-shell and trumpet resounds, as Indumati, in bridal robes, supported by Sunanda, is ushered in and stands in the walk left between them. It was delightful to dwell on the picture.

Then as Sunanda introduces to her each one of the suitors, Indumati bows low in loveless salutation, and passes on. How beautiful is this humble courtesy! They are all princes. They are all her seniors. For she is a mere girl. Had she not atoned for the inevitable rudeness of her rejection by the grace of her humility, the scene would have lost its beauty.

SHELIDAH,
20th August 1892.

"If only I could live there!" is often thought when looking at a beautiful landscape painting. That is the kind of longing which is satisfied here, where one feels alive in a brilliantly coloured picture, with none of the hardness of reality. When I was a child, illustrations of woodland and sea, in *Paul and Virginia*, or *Robinson Crusoe*, would waft me away from the everyday world; and the sunshine here brings back to my mind the feeling with which I used to gaze on those pictures.

I cannot account for this exactly, or explain definitely what kind of longing it is which is roused within me. It seems like the throb of some current flowing through the artery connecting me with the larger world. I feel as if dim, distant memories come to me of the time when I was one with the rest of the earth; when on me grew the green grass, and on me fell the autumn light; when a warm scent of youth would rise from every pore of my vast, soft, green body at the touch of the rays of the mellow sun, and a fresh life, a sweet joy, would be half-consciously secreted and inarticulately poured forth from all the immensity of my being, as it lay dumbly stretched, with its varied countries and seas and mountains, under the bright blue sky.

My feelings seem to be those of our ancient earth in the daily ecstasy of its sun-kissed life; my own consciousness seems to stream through each blade of grass, each sucking root, to rise with the sap through the trees, to break out with joyous thrills in the waving fields of corn, in the rustling palm leaves.

I feel impelled to give expression to my blood-tie with the earth, my kinsman's love for her; but I am afraid I shall not be understood.

BOALIA,
18*th November* 1892.

I am wondering where your train has got to by now. This is the time for the sun to rise over the ups and downs of the treeless, rocky region near Nawadih station. The scene around there must be brightened by the fresh sunlight, through which distant, blue hills are beginning to be faintly visible.

Cultivated fields are scarcely to be seen, except where the primitive tribesmen have done a little ploughing with their buffaloes; on each side of the railway cutting there are the heaped-up black rocks—the boulder-marked footprints of dried-up streams—and the fidgety, black wagtails, perched along the telegraph wires. A wild, seamed, and scarred nature lies there in the sun, as though tamed at the touch of some soft, bright, cherubic hand.

Do you know the picture which this calls up for me? In the *Sakuntala* of Kalidas there is a scene where Bharat, the infant son of King Dushyanta, is playing with a lion cub. The child is lovingly passing his delicate, rosy fingers through the rough mane of the great beast, which lies quietly stretched in trustful repose, now and then casting affectionate glances out of the corner of its eyes at its little human friend.

And shall I tell you what those dry, boulder-strewn watercourses put me in mind of? We read in the English fairy tale of the Babes in the Wood, how the little brother and sister left a trace of their wanderings, through the unknown forest into which their stepmother had turned them out, by dropping pebbles as they went. These streamlets are like lost babes in the great world into which they are sent adrift, and that is why they leave stones, as they go forth, to mark their course, so as not to lose their way when they may be returning. But for them there is no return journey!

NATORE,
2nd December 1892.

There is a depth of feeling and breadth of peace in a Bengal sunset behind the trees which fringe the endless solitary fields, spreading away to the horizon.

Lovingly, yet sadly withal, does our evening sky bend over and meet the earth in the distance. It casts a mournful light on the earth it leaves behind—a light which gives us a taste of the divine grief of the Eternal Separation;[1] and eloquent is the silence which then broods over earth, sky, and waters.

As I gaze on in rapt motionlessness, I fall to wondering.—If ever this silence should fail to contain itself, if the expression for which this hour has been seeking from the beginning of time should break forth, would a profoundly solemn, poignantly moving music rise from earth to starland?

With a little steadfast concentration of effort we can, for ourselves, translate

[1] *I.e.* between Purusha and Prakriti—God and Creation.

the grand harmony of light and colour which permeates the universe into music. We have only to close our eyes and receive with the ear of the mind the vibration of this ever-flowing panorama.

But how often shall I write of these sunsets and sunrises? I feel their renewed freshness every time; yet how am I to attain such renewed freshness in my attempts at expression?

SHELIDAH,
9th December 1892.

I am feeling weak and relaxed after my painful illness, and in this state the ministrations of nature are sweet indeed. I feel as if, like the rest, I too am lazily glittering out my delight at the rays of the sun, and my letter-writing progresses but absent-mindedly.

The world is ever new to me; like an old friend loved through this and former lives, the acquaintance between us is both long and deep.

I can well realise how, in ages past, when the earth in her first youth came forth from her sea-bath and saluted the sun in prayer, I must have been one of the trees sprung from her new-formed soil, spreading my foliage in all the freshness of a primal impulse.

The great sea was rocking and swaying and smothering, like a foolishly fond mother, its first-born land with repeated caresses; while I was drinking in the sunlight with the whole of my being, quivering under the blue sky with the unreasoning rapture of the new-born, holding fast and sucking away at my mother earth with all my roots. In blind joy my leaves burst forth and my flowers bloomed; and when the dark clouds gathered, their grateful shade would comfort me with a tender touch.

From age to age, thereafter, have I been diversely reborn on this earth. So whenever we now sit face to face, alone together, various ancient memories, gradually, one after another, come back to me.

My mother earth sits to-day in the cornfields by the river-side, in her raiment of sunlit gold; and near her feet, her knees, her lap, I roll about and play. Mother of a multitude of children, she attends but absently to their constant calls on her, with an immense patience, but also with a certain aloofness. She is seated there, with her far-away look fastened on the verge of the afternoon sky, while I keep chattering on untiringly.

BALIA,
Tuesday, February 1893.

I do not want to wander about any more. I am pining for a corner in which to nestle down snugly, away from the crowd.

India has two aspects—in one she is a householder, in the other a wandering ascetic. The former refuses to budge from the home corner, the latter has no home at all. I find both these within me. I want to roam about and see all the wide world, yet I also yearn for a little sheltered nook; like a bird with its tiny nest for a dwelling, and the vast sky for flight.

I hanker after a corner because it serves to bring calmness to my mind. My mind really wants to be busy, but in making the attempt it knocks so repeatedly against the crowd as to become utterly frenzied and to keep buffeting me, its cage, from within. If only it is allowed a little leisurely solitude, and can look about and think to its heart's content, it will express its feelings to its own satisfaction.

This freedom of solitude is what my mind is fretting for; it would be alone with its imaginings, as the Creator broods over His own creation.

CUTTACK,
February 1893.

Till we can achieve something, let us live incognito, say I. So long as we are only fit to be looked down upon, on what shall we base our claim to respect? When we have acquired a foothold of our own in the world, when we have had some share in shaping its course, then we can meet others smilingly. Till then let us keep in the background, attending to our own affairs.

But our countrymen seem to hold the opposite opinion. They set no store by our more modest, intimate wants which have to be met behind the scenes,—the whole of their attention is directed to momentary attitudinising and display.

Ours is truly a God-forsaken country. Difficult, indeed, is it for us to maintain the strength of will to *do*. We get no help in any real sense. There is no one, within miles of us, in converse with whom we might gain an accession of vitality. No one near seems to be thinking, or feeling, or working. Not a soul has any experience of big striving, or of really and truly living. They all eat and drink, do their office work, smoke and sleep, and chatter nonsensically. When they touch upon emotion they grow sentimental, when they reason they are childish. One yearns for a full-blooded, sturdy, and capable personality; these are all so many shadows, flitting about, out of touch with the world.

CUTTACK,
10th February 1893.

He was a fully developed John Bull of the outrageous type—with a huge beak of a nose, cunning eyes, and a yard-long chin. The curtailment of our right to be tried by jury is now under consideration by the Government. The fellow dragged in the subject by the ears and insisted on arguing it out with our host, poor B—— Babu. He said the moral standard of the people of this country was low; that they had no real belief in the sacredness of life; so that they were unfit to serve on juries.

The utter contempt with which we are regarded by these people was brought home to me when I saw how they can accept a Bengali's hospitality and talk thus, seated at his table, without a quiver of compunction.

As I sat in a corner of the drawing-room after dinner, everything round me looked blurred to my eyes. I seemed to be seated by the head of my great, insulted Motherland, who lay there in the dust before me, disconsolate, shorn of her glory. I cannot tell what a profound distress overpowered my heart.

How incongruous seemed the *mem-sahibs* there, in their evening-dresses, the hum of English conversation, and the ripples of laughter! How richly true for us is our India of the ages; how cheap and false the hollow courtesies of an English dinner-party!

CUTTACK,
March 1893.

If we begin to attach too much importance to the applause of Englishmen, we shall have to be rid of much in us that is good, and to accept from them much that is bad.

We shall grow ashamed of going about without socks, and cease to feel shame at the sight of their ball dresses. We shall have no compunction in throwing overboard our ancient manners, nor any in emulating their lack of courtesy.

We shall leave off wearing our *achgans* because they are susceptible of improvement, but think nothing of surrendering our heads to their hats, though no head-gear could well be uglier.

In short, consciously or unconsciously, we shall have to cut our lives down according as they clap their hands or not.

Wherefore I apostrophise myself and say: "O Earthen Pot! For goodness sake keep away from that Metal Pot! Whether he comes to you in anger or merely to give you a patronising pat on the back, you are done for, cracked in either case. So pay heed to old Æsop's sage counsel, I pray—and keep your distance."

Let the metal pot ornament wealthy homes; you have work to do in those of the poor. If you let yourself be broken, you will have no place in either, but merely return to the dust; or, at best, you may secure a corner in a bric-a-brac cabinet—as a curiosity, and it is more glorious far to be used for fetching water by the meanest of village women.

SHELIDAH,
8th May 1893.

Poetry is a very old love of mine—I must have been engaged to her when I was only Rathi's[1] age. Long ago the recesses under the old banyan tree beside our tank, the inner gardens, the unknown regions on the ground floor of the house, the whole of the outside world, the nursery rhymes and tales told by the maids, created a wonderful fairyland within me. It is difficult to give a clear idea of all the vague and mysterious happenings of that period, but this much is certain, that my exchange of garlands[2] with Poetic Fancy was already duly celebrated.

[1] Rathi, his son, was then five years old.
[2] The betrothal ceremony.

I must admit, however, that my betrothed is not an auspicious maiden—whatever else she may bring one, it is not good fortune. I cannot say she has never given me happiness, but peace of mind with her is out of the question. The lover whom she favours may get his fill of bliss, but his heart's blood is wrung out under her relentless embrace. It is not for the unfortunate creature of her choice ever to become a staid and sober householder, comfortably settled down on a social foundation.

Consciously or unconsciously, I may have done many things that were untrue, but I have never uttered anything false in my poetry—that is the sanctuary where the deepest truths of my life find refuge.

SHELIDAH,
10th May 1893.

Here come black, swollen masses of cloud; they soak up the golden sunshine from the scene in front of me like great pads of blotting-paper. Rain must be near, for the breeze feels moist and tearful.

Over there, on the sky-piercing peaks of Simla, you will find it hard to realise exactly what an important event the coming of the clouds is here, or how many are anxiously looking up to the sky, hailing their advent.

I feel a great tenderness for these peasant folk—our ryots—big, helpless, infantile children of Providence, who must have food brought to their very lips, or they are undone. When the breasts of Mother Earth dry up they are at a loss what to do, and can only cry. But no sooner is their hunger satisfied than they forget all their past sufferings.

I know not whether the socialistic ideal of a more equal distribution of wealth is attainable, but if not, the dispensation of Providence is indeed cruel, and man a truly unfortunate creature. For if in this world misery must exist, so be it; but let some little loophole, some glimpse of possibility at least, be left, which may serve to urge the nobler portion of humanity to hope and struggle unceasingly for its alleviation.

They say a terribly hard thing who assert that the division of the world's production to afford each one a mouthful of food, a bit of clothing, is only an Utopian dream. All these social problems are hard indeed! Fate has allowed humanity such a pitifully meagre coverlet, that in pulling it over one part of the world, another has to be left bare. In allaying our poverty we lose our wealth, and with this wealth what a world of grace and beauty and power is lost to us.

But the sun shines forth again, though

the clouds are still banked up in the West.

SHELIDAH,
11th May 1893.

There is another pleasure for me here. Sometimes one or other of our simple, devoted, old ryots comes to see me—and their worshipful homage is so unaffected! How much greater than I are they in the beautiful simplicity and sincerity of their reverence. What if I am unworthy of their veneration—their feeling loses nothing of its value.

I regard these grown-up children with the same kind of affection that I have for little children—but there is also a difference. They are more infantile still. Little children will grow up later on, but these big children never.

A meek and radiantly simple soul shines through their worn and wrinkled, old bodies. Little children are merely simple, they have not the unquestioning, unwavering devotion of these. If there be any undercurrent along which the souls of men may have communication with one another, then my sincere blessing will surely reach and serve them.

SHELIDAH,
16th May 1893.

I walk about for an hour on the river bank, fresh and clean after my afternoon bath. Then I get into the new jolly-boat, anchor in mid-stream, and on a bed, spread on the planked over-stern, I lie silently there on my back, in the darkness of the evening. Little S—— sits beside me and chatters away, and the sky becomes more and more thickly studded with stars.

Each day the thought recurs to me: Shall I be reborn under this star-spangled sky? Will the peaceful rapture of such wonderful evenings ever again be mine, on this silent Bengal river, in so secluded a corner of the world?

Perhaps not. The scene may be changed; I may be born with a different mind. Many such evenings may come, but they may refuse to nestle so trustfully, so lovingly, with such complete abandon, to my breast.

Curiously enough, my greatest fear is lest I should be reborn in Europe! For there one cannot recline like this with one's whole being laid open to the infinite above—one is liable, I am afraid, to be soundly rated for lying down at all. I should probably have been hustling strenuously in some factory or bank, or Parliament. Like the roads there, one's mind has to be stone-metalled for heavy traffic—geometrically laid out, and kept clear and regulated.

I am sure I cannot exactly say why this lazy, dreamy, self-absorbed, sky-filled state of mind seems to me the more desirable. I feel no whit inferior to the busiest men of the world as I lie here in my jolly-boat. Rather, had I girded up my loins to be strenuous, I might have seemed ever so feeble compared to those chips of old oaken blocks.

SHELIDAH,
3rd July 1893.

All last night the wind howled like a stray dog, and the rain still pours on without a break. The water from the fields is rushing in numberless, purling streams to the river. The dripping ryots are crossing the river in the ferry-boat, some with their tokas[1] on, others with yam leaves held over their heads. Big cargo-boats are gliding along, the boatman sitting drenched at his helm, the crew straining at the tow-ropes through the rain. The birds remain

[1] Conical hats of straw or of split bamboo.

gloomily confined to their nests, but the sons of men fare forth, for in spite of the weather the world's work must go on.

Two cowherd lads are grazing their cattle just in front of my boat. The cows are munching away with great gusto, their noses plunged into the lush grass, their tails incessantly busy flicking off the flies. The raindrops and the sticks of the cowherd boys fall on their backs with the same unreasonable persistency, and they bear both with equally uncritical resignation, steadily going on with their munch, munch, munch. These cows have such mild, affectionate, mournful eyes; why, I wonder, should Providence have thought fit to impose all the burden of man's work on the submissive shoulders of these great, gentle beasts?

The river is rising daily. What I could see yesterday only from the upper deck, I can now see from my cabin windows. Every morning I awake to find my field of vision growing larger. Not long since, only the tree-tops near those distant villages used to appear, like dark green clouds. To-day the whole of the wood is visible.

Land and water are gradually approaching each other like two bashful lovers. The limit of their shyness has nearly been reached—their arms will soon be round each other's necks. I shall enjoy my trip along this brimful river at the height of the rains. I am fidgeting to give the order to cast off.

SHELIDAH,
4th July 1893.

A little gleam of sunlight shows this morning. There was a break in the rains yesterday, but the clouds are banked up so heavily along the skirts of the sky that there is not much hope of the break lasting. It looks as if a heavy carpet of cloud had been rolled up to one side, and at any moment a fussy breeze may come along and spread it over the whole place again, covering every trace of blue sky and golden sunshine.

What a store of water must have been laid up in the sky this year. The river has already risen over the low *chur*-lands,[1] threatening to overwhelm all the standing crops. The wretched ryots, in despair, are cutting and bringing away in boats sheaves of half-ripe rice. As they pass my boat I hear them bewailing their fate. It is easy to understand how heart-rending it must be for cultivators to have to cut down their rice on the very eve of its ripening, the only hope left them being that some of the ears may possibly have hardened into grain.

[1] Old sand-banks consolidated by the deposit of a layer of culturable soil.

There must be some element of pity in the dispensations of Providence, else how did we get our share of it? But it is so difficult to see where it comes in. The lamentations of these hundreds of thousands of unoffending creatures do not seem to get anywhere. The rain pours on as it lists, the river still rises, and no amount of petitioning seems to have the effect of bringing relief from any quarter. One has to seek consolation by saying that all this is beyond the understanding of man. And yet, it is so vitally necessary for man to understand that there are such things as pity and justice in the world.

However, this is only sulking. Reason tells us that creation never can be perfectly happy. So long as it is incomplete it must put up with imperfection and sorrow. It can only be perfect when it ceases to be creation, and is God. Do our prayers dare go so far?

The more we think over it, the oftener we come back to the starting-point—Why this creation at all? If we cannot make up our minds to object to the thing itself, it is futile complaining about its companion, sorrow.

SHAZADPUR,
7th July 1893.

The flow of village life is not too rapid, neither is it stagnant. Work and rest go together, hand in hand. The ferry crosses to and fro, the passers-by with umbrellas up wend their way along the tow-path, women are washing rice on the split-bamboo trays which they dip in the water, the ryots are coming to the market with bundles of jute on their heads. Two men are chopping away at a log of wood with regular, ringing blows. The village carpenter is repairing an upturned dinghy under a big *aswatha* tree. A mongrel dog is prowling aimlessly along the canal bank. Some cows are lying there chewing the cud, after a huge meal off the luxuriant grass, lazily moving their ears backwards and forwards, flicking off flies with their tails, and occasionally giving an impatient toss of their heads when the crows perched on their backs take too much of a liberty.

The monotonous blows of wood-cutter's axe or carpenter's mallet, the splashing of oars, the merry voices of the naked little children at play, the plaintive tune of the ryot's song, the more dominant creaking of the turning oil-mill, all these sounds of activity do not seem out of harmony with murmuring leaves and singing birds, and all combine like moving strains of some grand dream-orchestra, rendering a composition of immense though restrained pathos.

SHAZADPUR,
10*th July* 1893.

All I have to say about the discussion that is going on over "silent poets" is that, though the strength of feeling may be the same in those who are silent as in those who are vocal, that has nothing to do with poetry. Poetry is not a matter of feeling, it is the creation of form.

Ideas take shape by some hidden, subtle skill at work within the poet. This creative power is the origin of poetry. Perceptions, feelings, or language, are only raw material. One may be gifted with feeling, a second with language, a third with both; but he who has as well a creative genius, alone is a poet.

PATISAR,
13*th August* 1893.

Coming through these *beels*[1] to Kali-

[1] *Translator's Note.*—Sometimes a stream passing through the flat Bengal country encounters a stretch

gram, an idea took shape in my mind. Not that the thought was new, but sometimes old ideas strike one with new force.

The water loses its beauty when it ceases to be defined by banks and spreads out into a monotonous vagueness. In the case of language, metre serves for banks and gives form and beauty and character. Just as the banks give each river a distinct personality, so does rhythm make each poem an indivi-

---

of low land and spreads out into a sheet of water, called a *beel*, of indefinite extent, ranging from a large pool in the dry season to a shoreless expanse during the rains.

Villages consisting of a cluster of huts, built on mounds, stand out here and there like islands, and boats or round, earthen vessels are the only means of getting about from village to village.

Where the waters cover cultivated tracts the rice grows through, often from considerable depths, giving to the boats sailing over them the curious appearance of gliding over a cornfield, so clear is the water. Elsewhere these *beels* have a peculiar flora and fauna of water-lilies and irises and various water-fowl. As a result, they resemble neither a marsh nor a lake, but have a distinct character of their own.

dual creation; prose is like the featureless, impersonal *beel*. Again, the waters of the river have movement and progress; those of the *beel* engulf the country by expanse alone. So, in order to give language power, the narrow bondage of metre becomes necessary; otherwise it spreads and spreads, but cannot advance.

The country people call these *beels* "dumb waters"—they have no language, no self-expression. The river ceaselessly babbles; so the words of the poem sing, they are not "dumb words." Thus bondage creates beauty of form, motion, and music; bounds make not only for beauty but power.

Poetry gives itself up to the control of metre, not led by blind habit, but because it thus finds the joy of motion. There are foolish persons who think that metre is a species of verbal gymnastics, or legerdemain, of which the object is to win the admiration of the crowd. That is not so. Metre is born as all beauty is born the universe through. The current set up within well-defined bounds gives metrical verse power to move the minds of men as vague and indefinite prose cannot.

This idea became clear to me as I glided on from river to *beel* and *beel* to river.

PATISAR,
26th (Straven) August 1893.

For some time it has struck me that man is a rough-hewn and woman a finished product.

There is an unbroken consistency in the manners, customs, speech, and adornment of woman. And the reason is, that for ages Nature has assigned to her the same definite rôle and has been adapting her to it. No cataclysm, no political revolution, no alteration of social ideal, has yet diverted woman from her particular functions, nor destroyed their inter-relations. She has loved, tended, and caressed, and done nothing else; and the exquisite skill which she has acquired in these, permeates all her being and doing. Her disposition and action have become inseparably one, like the flower and its scent. She has, therefore, no doubts or hesitations.

But the character of man has still many hollows and protuberances; each of the varied circumstances and forces which have contributed to his making has left its mark upon him. That is why the features of one will display an indefinite spread of forehead, of another an irresponsible prominence of nose, of a third an unaccountable hardness about the jaws. Had man but the benefit of continuity and uniformity of purpose, Nature must have succeeded in elaborating a definite mould for him, enabling him to function simply and naturally, without such strenuous effort. He would not have so complicated a code of behaviour; and he would be less liable to deviate from the normal when disturbed by outside influences.

Woman was cast in the mould of mother. Man has no such primal design to go by, and that is why he has been unable to rise to an equal perfection of beauty.

PATISAR,
19th February 1894.

We have two elephants which come to graze on this bank of the river. They greatly interest me. They give the ground a few taps with one foot, and then taking hold of the grass with the end of their trunks wrench off an enormous piece of turf, roots, soil, and all. This they go on swinging till all the earth leaves the roots; they then put it into their mouths and eat it up.

Sometimes the whim takes them to draw up the dust into their trunks, and then with a snort they squirt it all over their bodies; this is their elephantine toilet.

I love to look on these overgrown beasts, with their vast bodies, their immense strength, their ungainly proportions, their docile harmlessness. Their very size and clumsiness make me feel a kind of tenderness for them—their unwieldy bulk has something infantile about it. Moreover, they have large hearts. When they get wild they are furious, but when they calm down they are peace itself.

The uncouthness which goes with bigness does not repel, it rather attracts.

PATISAR,
27th February 1894.

The sky is every now and then overcast and again clears up. Sudden little puffs of wind make the boat lazily creak and groan in all its seams. Thus the day wears on.

It is now past one o'clock. Steeped in this countryside noonday, with its different sounds—the quacking of ducks, the swirl of passing boats, bathers splashing the clothes they wash, the distant shouts from drovers taking cattle across the ford,—it is difficult even to imagine the chair-and-table, monotonously dismal routine-life of Calcutta.

Calcutta is as ponderously proper as a Government office. Each of its days comes forth, like coin from a mint, clear-cut and glittering. Ah! those dreary, deadly days, so precisely equal in weight, so decently respectable!

Here I am quit of the demands of my circle, and do not feel like a wound-up machine. Each day is my own. And with leisure and my thoughts I walk the fields, unfettered by bounds of space or time. The evening gradually deepens over earth and sky and water, as with bowed head I stroll along.

PATISAR,
22nd March 1894.

As I was sitting at the window of the boat, looking out on the river, I saw, all of a sudden, an odd-looking bird making its way through the water to the opposite bank, followed by a great commotion. I found it was a domestic fowl which had managed to escape impending doom in the galley by jumping overboard and was now trying frantically to win across. It had almost gained the bank when the clutches of its relentless pursuers closed on it, and it was brought back in triumph, gripped by the neck. I told the cook I would not have any meat for dinner.

I really must give up animal food. We manage to swallow flesh only because we do not think of the cruel and sinful thing we do. There are many crimes which are the creation of man himself, the wrongfulness of which is put down to their divergence from habit, custom, or tradition. But cruelty is not of these. It is a fundamental sin, and admits of no argument or nice distinctions. If only we do not allow our heart to grow callous, its protest against cruelty is always clearly heard ; and yet we go on perpetrating cruelties easily, merrily, all of us—in fact, any one who does not join in is dubbed a crank.

How artificial is our apprehension of sin ! I feel that the highest commandment is that of sympathy for all sentient beings. Love is the foundation of all religion. The other day I read in one of the English papers that 50,000 pounds of animal carcasses had been sent to some army station in Africa, but the meat being found to have gone bad on arrival, the consignment was returned and was eventually auctioned off for a few pounds at Portsmouth. What a shocking waste of life! What callousness to its true worth! How many living creatures are sacrificed only to grace the dishes at a dinner-party, a large proportion of which will leave the table untouched!

So long as we are unconscious of our cruelty we may not be to blame. But if, after our pity is aroused, we persist in throttling our feelings simply in order to join others in their preying upon life, we insult all that is good in us. I have decided to try a vegetarian diet.

PATISAR,
28th March 1894.

It is getting rather warm here, but I do not mind the heat of the sun much. The heated wind whistles on its way, now and then pauses in a whirl, then dances away twirling its skirt of dust and sand and dry leaves and twigs.

This morning, however, it was quite cold—almost like a cold-weather morning; in fact, I did not feel over-enthusiastic for my bath. It is so difficult to account for what veritably happens in this big thing called Nature. Some obscure cause turns up in some unknown corner, and all of a sudden things look completely different.

The mind of man works in just the same mysterious fashion as outside Nature—so it struck me yesterday. A wondrous alchemy is being wrought in artery, vein, and nerve, in brain and marrow. The blood-stream rushes on, the nerve-strings vibrate, the heart-muscle rises and falls, and the seasons in man's being change from one to another. What kind of breezes will blow next, when and from what quarter —of that we know nothing.

One day I am sure I shall get along splendidly; I feel strong enough to leap over all the obstructing sorrows and trials of the world; and, as if I had a printed programme for the rest of my life tucked safely away in my pocket, I am at ease. The next day there is a nasty wind, sprung up from some unknown *inferno*, the aspect of the sky is threatening, and I begin to doubt whether I shall ever weather the storm. Merely because something has gone wrong in some blood-vessel or nerve-fibre, all my strength and intelligence seem to fail me.

This mystery within frightens me. It makes me diffident about talking of what I shall or shall not do. Why was this tacked on to me—this immense mystery which I can neither understand nor control? I know not where it may lead me or I lead it. I cannot see what is happening, nor am I consulted about what is going to happen, and yet I have to keep up an appearance of mastery and pretend to be the doer. . . .

I feel like a living pianoforte with a vast complication of machinery and wires inside, but with no means of telling who the player is, and with only a guess as to why the player plays at all. I can only know what is being played, whether the mode is merry or mournful, when the notes are sharp or flat, the tune in or out of time, the key high-pitched or low. But do I really know even that?

PATISAR,
30th March 1894.

Sometimes when I realise that Life's journey is long, and that the sorrows to be encountered are many and inevitable, a supreme effort is required to keep up my strength of mind. Some evenings, as I sit alone staring at the flame of the lamp on the table, I vow I will live as a brave man should—unmoved, silent, uncomplaining. The resolve puffs me up, and for the moment I mistake myself for a very, very brave person indeed. But as soon as the thorns on the road worry my feet, I writhe and begin to feel serious misgivings as to the future. The path of life again seems long, and my strength inadequate.

But this last conclusion cannot be the true one, for it is these petty thorns which are the most difficult to bear. The household of the mind is a thrifty one, and only so much is spent as is necessary. There is no squandering on trifles, and its wealth of strength is saved up with miserly strictness to meet the really big calamities. So any amount of weeping and wailing over the lesser griefs fails to evoke a charitable response. But when sorrow is deepest there is no stint of effort. Then the surface crust is pierced, and consolation wells up, and all the forces of patience and courage are banded together to do their duty. Thus great suffering brings with it the power of great endurance.

One side of man's nature has the desire for pleasure—there is another side which desires self-sacrifice. When the former meets with disappointment, the latter gains strength, and on its thus finding fuller scope a grand enthusiasm fills the soul. So while we are cowards before petty troubles, great sorrows make us brave by rousing our truer manhood. And in these, therefore, there is a joy.

It is not an empty paradox to say that there is joy in sorrow, just as, on the other hand, it is true that there is a dissatisfaction in pleasure. It is not difficult to understand why this should be so.

SHELIDAH,
24th June 1894.

I have been only four days here, but, having lost count of the hours, it seems such a long while, I feel that if I were to return to Calcutta to-day I should find much of it changed—as if I alone had been standing still outside the current of time, unconscious of the gradually changing position of the rest of the world.

The fact is that here, away from Calcutta, I live in my own inner world, where the clocks do not keep ordinary time ; where duration is measured only by the intensity of the feelings ; where, as the outside world does not count the minutes, moments change into hours and hours into moments. So it seems to me that the subdivisions of time and space are only mental illusions. Every atom is immeasurable and every moment infinite.

There is a Persian story which I was greatly taken with when I read it as a boy—I think I understood, even then, something of the underlying idea, though I was a mere child. To show the illusory character of time, a *faquir* put some magic water into a tub and asked the King to take a dip. The King no sooner dipped his head in than he found himself in a strange country by the sea, where he spent a good long time going through a variety of happenings and doings. He married, had children, his wife and children died, he lost all his wealth, and as he writhed under his sufferings he suddenly found himself back in the room, surrounded by his courtiers. On his proceeding to revile the *faquir* for his misfortunes, they said: "But, Sire, you have only just dipped your head in, and raised it out of the water!"

The whole of our life with its pleasures

and pains is in the same way enclosed in one moment of time. However long or intense we may feel it to be while it lasts, as soon as we have finished our dip in the tub of the world, we shall find how like a slight, momentary dream the whole thing has been. . . .

SHELIDAH,
9th August 1894.

I saw a dead bird floating down the current to-day. The history of its death may easily be divined. It had a nest in some mango tree at the edge of a village. It returned home in the evening, nestling there against soft-feathered companions, and resting a wearied little body in sleep. All of a sudden, in the night, the mighty Padma tossed slightly in her bed, and the earth was swept away from the roots of the mango tree. The little creature bereft of its nest awoke just for a moment before it went to sleep again for ever.

When I am in the presence of the awful mystery of all-destructive Nature, the difference between myself and the other living things seems trivial. In town, human society is to the fore and looms large; it is cruelly callous to the happiness and misery of other creatures as compared with its own.

In Europe, also, man is so complex and so dominant, that the animal is too merely an animal to him. To Indians the idea of the transmigration of the soul from animal to man, and man to animal, does not seem strange, and so from our scriptures pity for all sentient creatures has not been banished as a sentimental exaggeration.

When I am in close touch with Nature in the country, the Indian in me asserts itself and I cannot remain coldly indifferent to the abounding joy of life throbbing within the soft down-covered breast of a single tiny bird.

SHELIDAH,
10th August 1894.

Last night a rushing sound in the water awoke me—a sudden boisterous disturbance of the river current—probably the onslaught of a freshet: a thing that often happens at this season. One's feet on the planking of the boat become aware of a variety of forces at work beneath it. Slight tremors, little rockings, gentle heaves, and sudden jerks, all keep me in touch with the pulse of the flowing stream.

There must have been some sudden excitement in the night, which sent the current racing away. I rose and sat by the window. A hazy kind of light made the turbulent river look madder than ever. The sky was spotted with clouds. The reflection of a great big star quivered on the waters in a long streak, like a burning gash of pain. Both banks were vague with the dimness of slumber, and between them was this wild, sleepless unrest, running and running regardless of consequences.

To watch a scene like this in the middle of the night makes one feel altogether a different person, and the daylight life an illusion. Then again, this morning, that midnight world faded away into some dreamland, and vanished into thin air. The two are so different, yet both are true for man.

The day-world seems to me like European Music—its concords and discords resolving into each other in a great progression of harmony; the night-world like Indian Music—pure, unfettered melody, grave and poignant. What if their contrast be so striking—both move us. This principle of opposites is at the very root of creation, which is divided between the rule of the King and the Queen; Night and Day; the One and the Varied; the Eternal and the Evolving.

We Indians are under the rule of Night. We are immersed in the Eternal, the One. Our melodies are to be sung alone, to oneself; they take us out of the everyday world into a solitude aloof. European Music is for the multitude and takes them along, dancing, through the ups and downs of the joys and sorrows of men.

SHELIDAH,
13th August 1894.

Whatever I truly think, truly feel, truly realise,—its natural destiny is to find true expression. There is some force in me which continually works towards that end, but is not mine alone,—it permeates the universe. When this universal force is manifested within an individual, it is beyond his control and acts according to its own nature; and in surrendering our lives to its power is our greatest joy. It not only gives us expression, but also sensitiveness and love; this makes our feelings so fresh to us every time, so full of wonder.

When my little daughter delights me, she merges into the original mystery of joy which is the Universe; and my loving caresses are called forth like worship. I am sure that all our love is but worship of the Great Mystery, only we perform it unconsciously. Otherwise it is meaningless.

Like universal gravitation, which governs large and small alike in the world of matter, this universal joy exerts its attraction throughout our inner world, and baffles our understanding when we see it in a partial view. The only rational explanation of why we find joy in man and nature is given in the Upanishad :

> For of joy are born all created things.

SHELIDAH,
19th August 1894.

The Vedanta seems to help many to free their minds from all doubt as to the Universe and its First Cause, but my doubts remain undispelled. It is true that the Vedanta is simpler than most other theories. The problem of Creation and its Creator is more complex than appears at first sight ; but the Vedanta has certainly simplified it half way, by cutting the Gordian knot and leaving out Creation altogether.

There is only Brahma, and the rest of us merely imagine that we are,—it is wonderful how the human mind should have found room for such a thought. It is still more wonderful to think that the idea is not so inconsistent as it sounds, and the real difficulty is, rather, to prove that anything does exist.

Anyhow, when as now the moon is up, and with half-closed eyes I am stretched beneath it on the upper deck, the soft breeze cooling my problem-vexed head, then the earth, waters, and sky around, the gentle rippling of the river, the casual wayfarer passing along the tow-path, the occasional dinghy gliding by, the trees across the fields, vague in the moonlight, the sleepy village beyond, bounded by the dark shadows of its groves,—verily seem an illusion of *Maya*; and yet they cling to and draw the mind and heart more truly than truth itself, which is abstraction, and it becomes impossible to realise what kind of salvation there can be in freeing oneself from them.

SHAZADPUR,
5th September 1894.

I realise how hungry for space I have become, and take my fill of it in these rooms where I hold my state as sole monarch, with all doors and windows thrown open. Here the desire and power to write are mine as they are nowhere else. The stir of outside life comes into me in waves of verdure, and with its light and scent and sound stimulated my fancy into story-writing.

The afternoons have a special enchantment of their own. The glare of the sun, the silence, the solitude, the bird cries, especially the cawings of crows, and the delightful, restful leisure—these conspire to carry me away altogether.

Just such noondays seem to have gone to the making of the Arabian Nights,—in Damascus, Bokhara, or Samarkhand, with their desert roadways, files of camels, wandering horsemen, crystal springs, welling up under the shade of feathery date groves ; their wilderness of roses, songs of nightingales, wines of Shiraz ; their narrow bazaar paths with bright overhanging canopies, the men, in loose robes and multi-coloured turbans, selling dates and nuts and melons ; their palaces, fragrant with incense, luxurious with kincob-covered divans and bolsters by the window-side ; their Zobedia or Amina or Sufia with gaily decorated jacket, wide trousers, and gold-embroidered slippers, a long narghilah pipe curled up at her feet, with gorgeously liveried eunuchs on guard,—and all the possible and impossible tales of human deeds and desires, and the laughter and wailing, of that distant mysterious region.

ON THE WAY TO DIGHAPATIAYA,
20th September 1894.

Big trees are standing in the flood water, their trunks wholly submerged, their branches and foliage bending over the waters. Boats are tied up under shady groves of mango and bo tree, and people bathe screened behind them. Here and there cottages stand out in the current, their inner quadrangles under water.

As my boat rustles its way through standing crops it now and then comes across what was a pool and is still to be distinguished by its clusters of water-lilies, and diver-birds pursuing fish.

The water has penetrated every possible place. I have never before seen such a complete defeat of the land. A little more and the water will be right inside the cottages, and their occupants will have to put up *machans* to live on. The cows will die if they have to remain standing like this in water up to their knees. All the snakes have been flooded out of their holes, and they, with sundry other homeless reptiles and insects, will have to chum with man and take refuge on the thatch of his roof.

The vegetation rotting in the water, refuse of all kinds floating about, naked children with shrivelled limbs and enlarged spleens splashing everywhere, the long-suffering patient housewives exposed in their wet clothes to wind and rain, wading through their daily tasks with tucked-up skirts, and over all a thick pall of mosquitoes hovering in the noxious atmosphere—the sight is hardly pleasing!

Colds and fevers and rheumatism in every home, the malaria-stricken infants constantly crying,—nothing can save them. How is it possible for men to live in such unlovely, unhealthy, squalid, neglected surroundings? The fact is we are so used to bear everything, hands down,—the ravages of Nature, the oppression of rulers, the pressure of our *shastras* to which we have not a word to say, while they keep eternally grinding us down.

ON THE WAY TO BOALIA,
22nd September 1894.

It feels strange to be reminded that only thirty-two Autumns have come and gone in my life; for my memory seems to have receded back into the dimness of time immemorial; and when my inner world is flooded with a light, as of an unclouded autumn morning, I feel I am sitting at the window of some magic palace, gazing entranced on a scene of distant reminiscence, soothed with soft breezes laden with the faint perfume of all the Past.

Goethe on his death-bed wanted "more light." If I have any desire left at all at such a time, it will be for "more space" as well; for I dearly love both light and space. Many look down on Bengal as being only a flat country, but that is just what makes me revel in its scenery all the more. Its unobstructed sky is filled to the brim, like an amethyst cup, with the descending twilight and peace of the evening; and the golden skirt of the still, silent noonday spreads over the whole of it without let or hindrance.

Where is there another such country for the eye to look on, the mind to take in?

CALCUTTA,
5th October 1894.

To-morrow is the Durga Festival. As I was going to S——'s yesterday, I noticed images being made in almost every big house on the way. It struck me that during these few days of the Poojahs, old and young alike had become children.

When we come to think of it, all preparation for enjoyment is really a playing with toys which are of no consequence in themselves. From outside it may appear wasteful, but can that be called futile which raises such a wave of feeling through and through the country? Even the driest of worldly-wise people are moved out of their self-centred interests by the rush of the pervading emotion.

Thus, once every year there comes a period when all minds are in a melting mood, fit for the springing of love and affection and sympathy. The songs of welcome and farewell to the goddess, the meeting of loved ones, the strains of the festive pipes, the limpid sky and molten gold of autumn, are all parts of one great paean of joy.

Pure joy is the children's joy. They have the power of using any and every trivial thing to create their world of interest, and the ugliest doll is made beautiful with their imagination and lives with their life. He who can retain this faculty of enjoyment after he has grown up, is indeed the true Idealist. For him things are not merely visible to the eye or audible to the ear, but they are also sensible to the heart, and their narrowness and imperfections are lost in the glad music which he himself supplies.

Every one cannot hope to be an Idealist, but a whole people approaches nearest to this blissful state at such seasons of festivity. And then what may ordinarily appear to be a mere toy loses its limitations and becomes glorified with an ideal radiance.

BOLPUR,
19th October 1894.

We know people only in dotted outline, that is to say, with gaps in our knowledge which we have to fill in ourselves, as best we can. Thus, even those we know well are largely made up of our imagination. Sometimes the lines are so broken, with even the guiding dots missing, that a portion of the picture remains darkly confused and uncertain. If, then, our best friends are only pieces of broken outline strung on a thread of imagination, do we really know anybody at all, or does anybody know us except in the same disjointed fashion? But perhaps it is these very loopholes, allowing entrance to each other's imagination, which make for intimacy; otherwise each one, secure in his inviolate individuality, would have been unapproachable to all but the Dweller within.

Our own self, too, we know only in bits, and with these scraps of material we have to shape the hero of our life-story,—likewise with the help of our imagination. Providence has, doubtless, deliberately omitted portions so that we may assist in our own creation.

BOLPUR,
31st October 1894.

The first of the north winds has begun to blow to-day, shiveringly. It looks as if there had been a visitation of the tax-gatherer in the *Amlaki* groves,—everything beside itself, sighing, trembling, withering. The tired impassiveness of the noonday sunshine, with its monotonous cooing of doves in the dense shade of the mango-tops, seems to overcast the drowsy watches of the day with a pang, as of some impending parting.

The ticking of the clock on my table, and the pattering of the squirrels which scamper in and out of my room, are in harmony with all other midday sounds.

It amuses me to watch these soft,

grey and black striped, furry squirrels, with their bushy tails, their twinkling bead-like eyes, their gentle yet busily practical demeanour. Everything eatable has to be put away in the wire-gauze cupboard in the corner, safe from these greedy creatures. So, sniffing with an irrepressible eagerness, they come nosing round and round the cupboard, trying to find some hole for entrance. If any grain or crumb has been dropped outside they are sure to find it, and, taking it between their forepaws, nibble away with great industry, turning it over and over to adjust it to their mouths. At the least movement of mine up go their tails over their backs and off they run, only to stop short half-way, sit up on their tails on the door-mat, scratching their ears with their hind-paws, and then come back.

Thus little sounds continue all day long—gnawing teeth, scampering feet, and the tinkling of the china on the shelves.

SHELIDAH,
7th December 1894.

As I walk on the moonlit sands, S—— usually comes up for a business talk.

He came last evening; and when silence fell upon me after the talk was over, I became aware of the eternal universe standing before me in the evening light. The trivial chatter of one person had been enough to obscure the presence of its all-pervading manifestation.

As soon as the patter of words came to an end, the peace of the stars descended, and filled my heart to overflowing. I found my seat in one corner, with these assembled millions of shining orbs, in the great mysterious conclave of Being.

I have to start out early in the evening so as to let my mind absorb the tranquillity outside, before S—— comes along with his jarring inquiries as to whether the milk has agreed with me, and if I have finished going through the Annual Statement.

How curiously placed are we between the Eternal and the Ephemeral! Any allusion to the affairs of the stomach sounds so hopelessly discordant when the mind is dwelling on the things of the spirit,—and yet the soul and the stomach have been living together so long. The very spot on which the moonlight falls is my landed property, but the moonlight tells me that my *zamindari* is an illusion, and my *zamindari* tells me that this moonlight is all emptiness. And as for poor me, I remain distracted between the two.

SHELIDAH,
23rd February 1895.

I grow quite absent-minded when I try to write for the *Sadhana* magazine.

I raise my eyes to every passing boat and keep staring at the ferry going to and fro. And then on the bank, close to my boat, there are a herd of buffaloes thrusting their massive snouts into the herbage, wrapping their tongues round it to get it into their mouths, and then munching away, blowing hard with great big gasps of contentment, and flicking the flies off their backs with their tails.

All of a sudden a naked weakling of a human cub appears on the scene, makes sundry noises, and pokes one of the patient beasts with a cudgel, whereupon, throwing occasional glances at the human sprig out of a corner of its eye, and snatching at tufts of leaves or grass here and there on the way, the unruffled beast leisurely moves on a few paces, and that imp of a boy seems to feel that his duty as herdsman has been done.

I fail to penetrate this mystery of the boy-cowherd's mind. Whenever a cow or a buffalo has selected a spot to its liking and is comfortably grazing there, I cannot divine what purpose is served by worrying it, as he insists on doing, till it shifts somewhere else. I suppose it is man's masterfulness glorying in triumph over the powerful creature it has tamed. Anyhow, I love to see these buffaloes amongst the lush grass.

But this is not what I started to say. I wanted to tell you how the least thing distracts me nowadays from my duty to the *Sadhana*. In my last letter[1] I told you of the bumble-bees which hover round me in some fruitless quest, to the tune of a meaningless humming, with tireless assiduity.

They come every day at about nine or ten in the morning, dart up to my table, shoot down under the desk, go

[1] Not included in this selection.

bang on to the coloured glass window-pane, and then with a circuit or two round my head are off again with a whizz.

I could easily have thought them to be departed spirits who had left this world unsatisfied, and so keep coming back to it again and again in the guise of bees, paying me an inquiring visit in passing. But I think nothing of the kind. I am sure they are real bees, otherwise known, in Sanskrit, as honey-suckers, or on still rarer occasions as double-proboscideans.

SHELIDAH,
16*th* (*Phalgun*) *February* 1895.

We have to tread every single moment of the way as we go on living our life, but when taken as a whole it is such a very small thing, two hours uninterrupted thought can hold all of it.

After thirty years of strenuous living

Shelley could only supply material for two volumes of biography, of which, moreover, a considerable space is taken up by Dowden's chatter. The thirty years of my life would not fill even one volume.

What a to-do there is over this tiny bit of life! To think of the quantity of land and trade and commerce which go to furnish its commissariat alone, the amount of space occupied by each individual throughout the world, though one little chair is large enough to hold the whole of him! Yet, after all is over and done, there remains only material for two hours' thought, some pages of writing!

What a negligible fraction of my few pages would this one lazy day of mine occupy! But then, will not this peaceful day, on the desolate sands by the placid river, leave nevertheless a distinct little gold mark even upon the scroll of my eternal past and eternal future?

SHELIDAH,
28th February 1895.

I have got an anonymous letter today which begins:

> To give up one's self at the feet of another, is the truest of all gifts.

The writer has never seen me, but knows me from my writings, and goes on to say:

> However petty or distant, the Sun[1]-worshipper gets a share of the Sun's rays. You are the world's poet, yet to me it seems you are my own poet!

and more in the same strain.

Man is so anxious to bestow his love on some object, that he ends by falling in love with his own Ideal. But why should we suppose the idea to be less true than the reality? We can never know for certain the truth of the

[1] Rabi, the author's name, means the Sun.

substance underlying what we get through the senses. Why should the doubt be greater in the case of the entity behind the ideas which are the creation of mind?

The mother realises in her child the great Idea, which is in every child, the ineffableness of which, however, is not revealed to any one else. Are we to say that what draws forth the mother's very life and soul is illusory, but what fails to draw the rest of us to the same extent is the real truth?

Every person is worthy of an infinite wealth of love—the beauty of his soul knows no limit. . . . But I am departing into generalities. What I wanted to express is, that in one sense I have no right to accept this offering of my admirer's heart; that is to say, for me, seen within my everyday covering, such a person could not possibly have had these feelings. But there is another sense in which I am worthy of all this, or of even greater adoration.

On the Way to Pabna,
9th July 1895.

I am gliding through this winding little Ichamati, this streamlet of the rainy season. With rows of villages along its banks, its fields of jute and sugar-cane, its reed patches, its green bathing slopes, it is like a few lines of a poem, often repeated and as often enjoyed. One cannot commit to memory a big river like the Padma, but this meandering little Ichamati, the flow of whose syllables is regulated by the rhythm of the rains, I am gradually making my very own. . . .

It is dusk, the sky getting dark with clouds. The thunder rumbles fitfully, and the wild casuarina clumps bend in waves to the stormy gusts which pass through them. The depths of bamboo thickets look black as ink. The pallid twilight glimmers over the water like the herald of some weird event.

I am bending over my desk in the dimness, writing this letter. I want to whisper low-toned, intimate talk, in keeping with this penumbra of the dusk. But it is just wishes like these which baffle all effort. They either get fulfilled of themselves, or not at all. That is why it is a simple matter to warm up to a grim battle, but not to an easy, inconsequent talk.

SHELIDAH,
14th August 1895.

One great point about work is that for its sake the individual has to make light of his personal joys and sorrows; indeed, so far as may be, to ignore them. I am reminded of an incident at Shazadpur. My servant was late one morning, and I was greatly annoyed at his delay. He came up and stood before me with his usual *salaam*, and with a slight catch in his voice explained that his eight-year-old daughter had died last night. Then, with his duster, he set to tidying up my room.

When we look at the field of work, we see some at their trades, some tilling the soil, some carrying burdens, and yet underneath, death, sorrow, and loss are flowing, in an unseen undercurrent, every day,—their privacy not intruded upon. If ever these should break forth beyond control and come to the surface, then all this work would at once come to a stop. Over the individual sorrows, flowing beneath, is a hard stone track, across which the trains of duty, with their human load, thunder their way, stopping for none save at appointed stations. This very cruelty of work proves, perhaps, man's sternest consolation.

KUSHTEA,
5th October 1895.

The religion that only comes to us from external scriptures never becomes our own; our only tie with it is that of habit. To gain religion within is man's great lifelong adventure. In the extremity of suffering must it be born; on his life-blood it must live; and then, whether or not it brings him happiness, the man's journey shall end in the joy of fulfilment.

We rarely realise how false for us is that which we hear from other lips, or keep repeating with our own, while all the time the temple of our Truth is building within us, brick by brick, day after day. We fail to understand the mystery of this eternal building when we view our joys and sorrows apart by themselves, in the midst of fleeting time; just as a sentence becomes unintelligible if one has to spell through every word of it.

When once we perceive the unity of the scheme of that creation which is going on in us, we realise our relation to the ever-unfolding universe. We realise that we are in the process of being created in the same way as are the glowing heavenly orbs which revolve in their courses,—our desires, our sufferings, all finding their proper place within the whole.

We may not know exactly what is happening: we do not know exactly even about a speck of dust. But when we feel the flow of life in us to be one with the universal life outside, then all our pleasures and pains are seen strung upon one long thread of joy. The facts: *I am, I move, I grow*, are seen in all their immensity in connection with the fact that everything else is there along with me, and not the tiniest atom can do without me.

The relation of my soul to this beautiful autumn morning, this vast radiance, is one of intimate kinship; and all this colour, scent, and music is but the outward expression of our secret communion. This constant communion, whether realised or unrealised, keeps my mind in movement; out of this intercourse between my inner and outer worlds I gain such religion, be it much or little, as my capacity allows: and in its light I have to test scriptures before I can make them really my own.

SHELIDAH,
12th December 1895.

The other evening I was reading an English book of criticisms, full of all manner of disputations about Poetry, Art, Beauty, and so forth and so on. As I plodded through these artificial discussions, my tired faculties seemed to have wandered into a region of empty mirage, filled with the presence of a mocking demon.

The night was far advanced. I closed the book with a bang and flung it on the table. Then I blew out the lamp with the idea of turning into bed. No sooner had I done so than, through the open windows, the moonlight burst into the room, with a shock of surprise.

That little bit of a lamp had been sneering drily at me, like some Mephistopheles: and that tiniest sneer had screened off this infinite light of joy issuing forth from the deep love which is in all the world. What, forsooth, had I been looking for in the empty wordiness of the book? There was the very thing itself, filling the skies, silently waiting for me outside, all these hours!

If I had gone off to bed leaving the

shutters closed, and thus missed this vision, it would have stayed there all the same without any protest against the mocking lamp inside. Even if I had remained blind to it all my life,—letting the lamp triumph to the end,—till for the last time I went darkling to bed,—even then the moon would have still been there, sweetly smiling, unperturbed and unobtrusive, waiting for me as she has throughout the ages.

THE END